988

To Georgia,
Thanks for all
your help and encourage
ment!

love,
Mary Ann

D043660?

THE

EQUALITY

TRAP

MARY ANN MASON

SIMON AND SCHUSTER

NEW YORK · LONDON · TORONTO · SYDNEY · TOKYO

SIMON AND SCHUSTER
Simon & Schuster Building
Rockefeller Center
1230 Avenue of the Americas
New York, New York 10020

Copyright © 1988 by Mary Ann Mason
All rights reserved
including the right of reproduction
in whole or in part in any form.
SIMON AND SCHUSTER and colophon are
registered trademarks of Simon & Schuster Inc.

Designed by Edith Fowler
Manufactured in the United States of America

10 9 8 7 6 5 4 3 2

Library of Congress Cataloging in Publication Data
Mason, Mary Ann.

The equality trap / Mary Ann Mason.
     p.   cm.
Bibliography: p.
ISBN 0–671–61715–X
    1. Divorced mothers—United States—Social conditions.
2. Divorced mothers—Employment—United States.
3. Working mothers—Employment—United States.   I. Title.
HQ834.M33   1988   88–11414
306.8′9–dc 19   CIP
ISBN 0–671–61715–X

ACKNOWLEDGMENTS

The stories of the women I relate in this book are a small fraction of the women whose stories have inspired this undertaking. The names and situations of the women whose stories I do use have been altered to protect their privacy. I thank them for sharing their lives.

Many friends and colleagues have assisted me by their thoughtful reading of parts of the manuscript in progress. They gave me both emotional and practical support. Often at a point where I was weary and losing confidence as well as energy, a reader would call and say something like "You've really got your finger on something, but . . ." It was the positive response that kept me going, and the "but" that made me take yet another hard look at what I had written. These are some of my kind critics (in alphabetical order): Rachel Bradley, Jo Carson, Karen Faircloth, Neil and Barbara Gilbert, Laura Karstensen, Annette Lawson, Bogna Lorence Kott, Madeline McLaughlin, Linda Mihaley, Clark Moscrip, Linda and George Moss, Maureen O'Sullivan, Sally and Bob Ornstein, Mindy Thomas, Leslie Zwillinger.

I am particularly indebted to Dr. Judith Wallerstein for sharing information on custody and divorce not available in print.

Special thanks to my research assistant, Carli Hegli, who showed equal proficiency in finding information in the law library and the popular-magazine stacks.

I am grateful to my agent, Carol Mann, who showed enthusiasm in the project when it was still a glimmer in my mind, and to my editors at Simon and Schuster, Jane Isay and Bob Bender, whose intelligent criticisms prompted revisions that were not always welcomed but were always right.

My best editor and critic has been my husband, Paul Ekman. Every one of the ideas and every page of the text have been scrutinized and improved by his sharp probing. This level of attention could only be considered a work of love, which it was.

I thank my children, Tom and Eve. They are the reason I wrote this book.

FOR PAUL

CONTENTS

INTRODUCTION:
THE BIRTH OF AN IDEA

I am stopped dead on the San Francisco Bay Bridge. I
shut off the engine; I have not moved for twenty minutes. The minutes and then the hours tick by. My heart
beats faster and louder as I stare at the dashboard
clock. I was due to pick up my four-year-old son at five
o'clock. The hands are crawling past six o'clock, seven
o'clock, eight o'clock. Finally the cars break free and I
race to the baby-sitter's house. She primly informs me
that she had no idea where I was and she has called
the police to take my son. Choking with anxiety, I drive
to the police station. The cruel-mouthed sergeant tells
me that my son has been sent to his father. The police
have determined that I am clearly not a fit mother and
will no longer be allowed to take care of him.

This is my recurring nightmare. It is founded in a

real incident which occurred ten years ago when I was living through a painful divorce and trying to learn the difficult role of single-parent working mother. The real-life incident did not end disastrously; the baby-sitter was merely annoyed. But clearly the sharp anxiety and profound feelings of inadequacy which were evoked by that very troubled period have not yet been put to rest.

The recurrence of this nightmare always reminds me that no matter how calmly and logically we present our ideas, they do not descend upon us as pure thoughts. I have wrestled with the concept of equality between men and women for more than twenty years. My understanding of equality and its consequences has been shaped as much by my evolving role as student, wife, mother, single parent, working mother as it has by my professional activities as a labor historian and lawyer. But it was the wrenching experience of divorce that has most profoundly affected the way in which I have come to see the problem of equality.

When I arrived in California in the late sixties with an almost completed Ph.D. in American history, the idea of complete equality between the sexes seemed perfectly reasonable if not self-evident. At that point it suited my life experience as well. I had graduated from an Eastern women's college where I was taught that a competent self-confident woman could do anything a man could, and I had entered a marriage based on an explicit agreement to divide household chores evenly.

As soon as I landed my first teaching job, at a small women's college in Oakland, I eagerly introduced courses in women's history and black history and tried out the social theories I had learned in graduate school. I was particularly enamored with the analogy between slaves and wives in the nineteenth century. Both had acquired a dependent, even childlike personality (the

Sambo figure and the doll-wife) because they were treated as dependent children by their protective husbands/masters. Advancing this observation to the social turbulence of the sixties, I felt it was obvious that if blacks and women were treated exactly the same as the white men who still held the reins of power, they would grab those reins of power. Race and sex were simply part of a mind-set that allowed white men to dominate.

My young white women students were impressed by this theory, my black students were not. Members of the then notorious Black Panther Party, whose headquarters were just down the hill, occasionally came to talk to my classes, and they did not want to be compared with women. They believed the analogy was implicitly racist.

I completed my Ph.D., with a specialty in labor history, bore my first child, and found myself jobless. This, at least, was not a product of discrimination, since there were no jobs for fresh Ph.D.s in history, men or women, in 1972. But of course, as a new mother and the wife of an employed academic, I could not leave the San Francisco Bay Area to follow a job.

Like many unemployed Ph.D.s of that era, I chose to return to law school. I made the difficult but not impossible child-care arrangements without complaint, and rarely mentioned my toddler in the company of my fellow law students. The flexibility of student life allowed me to spend a good deal of time at home, and I saw little problem in handling motherhood and career. It seemed clearly possible to do it all. I took for granted the support of my husband, who both paid the rent and took care of our little boy during exams.

The jarring and irreparable blow to my ideal of equality between the sexes occurred when my marriage of twelve years ended, shortly after I had completed law school. The marriage ended for all the modern reasons: finding oneself, outgrowing each other, etc.

This was California in the mid-seventies, and I experienced, with firsthand pain, the effect of the new no-fault laws I had studied in law school: no contest, no alimony, minimal child support, and assets cut down the middle, which for most women meant sale of the family home and a move downhill to a small apartment. I learned quickly that working full time as a lawyer with the responsibilities of a single parent was a vast universe away from being a student mother with a husband. Getting through each day, simple survival, was all I could manage.

Both by chance and by choice I became a family-law practitioner; that is, I got women through their divorces. Everyone had her story, and most were far worse than mine. Many of my clients had been working full time before the divorce to build a livable family wage between two people. Their income alone could not support their own lives, let alone the children for whom they inevitably became totally responsible. Some of these formerly solid middle-class wives found themselves asking for food stamps and Medi-Cal, the health insurance for the poor.

These painful life experiences forced me to reexamine all my beliefs regarding men and women. What was it that I and all my clients had lost? We had lost the support of our husbands, and we had lost the protection of laws that were supposed to come to the aid of women and children in times of crisis. That hateful word, "protection," which I had been confident created only dependence and timidity, I now saw in a different light.

It occurred to me that I as much as anyone, and more than most, was responsible for creating a climate of opinion which proudly declared that women could take care of themselves as well as men could, and that the union of a man and a woman was an egalitarian arrangement which could be ended at the whim of either. This simply did not work when women had children. A family with children is not an egalitarian arrangement but rather a mutual-support society where all the members, children and father as well as mother, depended upon one another for emotional support and physical protection from the outside world. The degree of each member's contribution varies with age and over time, but nobody keeps score.

I looked anew at what was happening to women in the work world. While I turned my back to pursue law the entire American labor scene had been transformed. Married women with children were flooding into the labor force because their husbands were no longer earning a "family wage." The postwar shift away from a manufacturing economy and toward a service economy severely reduced the number of high-paying jobs for steelworkers while producing a vast number of low-paying jobs for file clerks. Not only could women get these jobs, employers preferred them over men, since they came cheap. Even women like me who had entered the male-dominated professions came relatively cheap. Because of our children we could not compete for the high-paying, high-pressure, time-intensive jobs.

Almost overnight, women have become the new immigrants. They are taking over the low rungs of the labor market, usurping the role played by generations of new immigrants who began their climb with these jobs. In a manufacturing economy new immigrants dug for iron ore and coal; in this service/information economy women process paper. Today's immigrants cannot even compete with women for these jobs, since they do not have the required language skills.

It struck me that the idea of equality for women has

worked well for the economy but not for women. In order to survive as an economic giant, America has had to lure women into the workplace at low wages. The egalitarian ideal glorifies work, even its meanest forms, for all women, including mothers, and it asks for no favors. It is clearly to the advantage of employers and the government to treat women as it treats men. The kinds of special consideration today's working mothers desperately need, maternity leaves, children's sick leave, flexible hours, part-time work with medical benefits, and child care, cost money. It costs little or nothing to hire a woman rather than a man as long as the woman does the same job as a man and asks for no special consideration.

I now understand the adamant opposition of most feminists of the 1920s and '30s, like Jane Addams and Florence Howe, to the Equal Rights Amendment. They grasped the fundamental truth that modern women have lost, that women need special consideration in their role as mothers. Equality is a two-edged sword that can cut women down as well as help them up. Equality works as a strategy only in the limited situations where women are actually in the same situation as men. It can therefore be a useful strategy for young women students, or for women who will not have children and wish to compete with men. Women with children will always get the sharp edge of the sword.

I wrote this book so that I could better understand, and hopefully help others better understand, the forces that shape American women's lives today; for surely there has never been a more confusing or troubled time for women in America. I have found that it is far easier to look into the past and analyze the mistakes of those who are long dead, as an historian, than to provide concrete strategies for new directions for the living.

Intellectually, my struggle with the idea of equality

between the sexes will surely go on, but personally I have made a separate peace. Unlike most of my divorce clients who are still single parents, I have had the good fortune to remarry, to have a second child and to enjoy the support and protection, as well as the responsibility, of a complete family. I have continued the difficult balancing act of full-time work and children, spending a good part of the last ten years working with reentry women in a paralegal program which I founded and continue to direct. I listen to and learn from these women, who represent all ages and backgrounds. Their stories have helped me articulate the ideas which are the foundation of this book. I have changed their names to protect their identities, but their voices come through clearly.

1

THE EQUALITY TRAP

Something has gone very wrong with the lives of women. Women are working much harder than they have worked in recent history, they are growing steadily poorer, and they are suffering the brutality of divorce at an unprecedented rate. The greatly publicized success of a very few women in high positions has created the illusion that the equal-rights crusade has dramatically improved the lives of all women. The reality is that the everyday quality of women's lives has gravely deteriorated.

Shouldering the double burden of work inside and outside the home, women are toiling longer and longer hours. For a working mother, the eighty-hour work week is now depressingly commonplace. Between 1959 and 1983 the collective number of hours that all women between twenty-five and sixty-four put into the marketplace nearly doubled, while the number of hours that they devoted to child care and housework decreased by only 14 percent. During this same period the total hours worked by men in the marketplace and at home combined *fell* by 8 percent.[1]

At work, women can now expect to earn about seventy cents for every dollar earned by men, a slight rise since 1939, when they earned sixty-three cents on the dollar.[2] The much heralded egalitarian legislation, Title VII of the 1964 Civil Rights Act, which prohibits discrimination against women in employment, and the Equal Pay Act of 1963, which mandates that men and women receive equal pay for the same task, have barely shaken this wage gap. And these figures do not tell the whole story. The shift from a manufacturing to a service economy has drastically reduced the paycheck brought home by the average worker. Between 1973 and 1985 the average weekly income of the typical worker fell by 13 percent.[3] The majority of men no longer earn a wage which will support a family. Men and women alike must run faster to earn more to stay in place.

Most women are flooding the workplace, not driven by the desire to become a corporate executive, but struggling to maintain a decent lifestyle for their families, or simply to survive as a single parent. These women are "working to live." They are filling the same female-dominated occupations that they have always filled, secretaries, clerks, food service workers, only in greater numbers than ever before. Equal opportunity to compete with men in the workplace has done them no good, since they are mainly competing with other women. For the swelling numbers of reentry women with musty or minimal skill, or for the part-time or casual women workers who are hanging on to the least skilled jobs, the chance to compete equally is meaningless, since they are not equipped with the skills to do so.

What about the woman corporate vice-president, or the first female law partner? They are the glamorous subjects of women's magazines, their stories are the fuel lighting the crusade toward equality, even though they represent a tiny percent of all working women. There is no doubt that the climate of egalitarian expectations has encouraged many women to try harder. These are the women who "live to work"; women whose highest priority is job success. For them the door has opened a crack in male-dominated occupations. The egalitarian push has prompted some institutions to create a chair or two in the boardroom for women or to raise a few women to top management.

The woman who "lives to work" does well until the baby arrives. The male working world has not changed its career clock to accommodate the needs of mothers; an executive or a lawyer is not expected to leave promptly at five to pick up a child at day care, or to stay home with a sick baby. And if the woman drops out of the career race even for a few years she will probably not be allowed to reenter. The egalitarian ideal of shared domestic chores inevitably falls apart at home. Even among couples who pledge an egalitarian union, women ultimately assume the vast bulk of what needs to be done. At best there is never enough help in this servantless era. Fatigue sets in, and the woman who "does it all" feels that she does it all badly.

But it is with courtship and marriage that the failure of the egalitarian crusade is most painfully experienced. The lives of millions of women and children have already been damaged by divorce, and the projection is that at least half of all marriages entered into today will end in the courts.[4] The divorce rate has more than doubled since 1959, propelled by the momentum of the new no-fault divorce laws which have stampeded through all states except South Dakota.

No-fault laws reflect the new egalitarian attitude toward divorce which has effectively replaced moral responsibility. Neither party is at fault, therefore no one is responsible for the end of a marriage.

Laws that protected women and children following divorce have been replaced by laws that dictate that women can take care of themselves as well as men can, even when they are also taking care of the children. The result of this egalitarian approach in California, the pioneer of no-fault divorce, is that a woman can expect a 73 percent drop in disposable income one year after divorce, while her ex-husband experiences a 42 percent increase.[5] Poor women get poorer, and comfortably middle-class women can suddenly fall into threadbare survival or even public dependency. A staggering 54 percent of single-parent families now live below the poverty line; more than 90 percent of these are headed by women.[6] Divorce is not the only factor creating this new class of poor women and children, but it is a major contributor.

An egalitarian approach is being widely adopted to divide children upon divorce as well. Laws that looked to the "best interests of the children" are being abandoned to accommodate an equal division of both children and property. Without study or consideration, and even without the consent of the parents, fifty-fifty custody arrangements are being ordered in many states. This can have drastic effects on the children whose lives are cut in half. Women, who have traditionally been the guardians and protectors of the rights of children, have allowed this to happen while they focused their attention on success in the marketplace.

Divorce is the final collapse of the crumbling relationship between men and women, but the fissures are evident during courtship. Women of all ages complain about the lack of commitment of modern men. There is a dearth of "family men" like their fathers and uncles; men who settled into lifelong loyalty. Men feel that women have given them the clear message that independence is the liberated woman's goal. Equality between the sexes quickly breaks down into each man/woman for himself/herself, shattering the delicate symbiotic ties that bind men and women together. Each sex blames the other, not understanding that they both are caught in a larger net of social change.

Sexual equality, as opposed to equality between the sexes, further weakens the bonds between men and women. Sex has become a competitive sport in which continual conquests are the goal. Women, more often and sooner than men, want to abandon this game in order to raise children and build security. Men can simply find new playmates.

How did women get themselves into this fix? How can so many women sustain the illusion of progress if in fact their condition is deteriorating? Ironically, the failure to obtain passage of the Equal Rights Amendment, the capstone of the egalitarian crusade, delayed for more than a decade a realization of what was actually happening to women.

The real revolution in women's lives would have occurred whether or not there had been a feminist movement with its crusade for equal rights. The real revolution in the United States has been an economic revolution that requires women to work to maintain a family in the face of declining living wages. A young woman must expect to spend the whole of her adult life in the work force, taking little or no break for the demands of motherhood. This is the mandate of an apparently affluent economy which needs ever more

workers at low wages to maintain the illusion of af-
fluence.

The revolution occurred almost without note. Inflation helped to obscure the fact that a man's paycheck
could no longer support the family. The good-paying
jobs in the highly unionized manufacturing sector slowly
dissolved, while the want ads screamed for secretaries.
The woman who had expected to abandon her type-
writer for the kitchen and the nursery was obliged to
stay on to save for the house, and then found it necessary to stay on once the children were born in order
to pay for the house. Too often she stayed on after the
man had left the house, leaving her to support both
the house and the children.

Beginning in the late sixties the American economy
churned out more and more new jobs, twenty million
between 1974 and 1984 alone, providing the illusion
of a prosperous, expanding economy even though real
wages were shrinking. The vast majority of these new
jobs were in the amorphous service/information sector,
which covers a wide range from fast-food attendant to
word processor.[7] What these new jobs almost all had
in common were lower pay, fewer benefits, and less
security than those in the declining manufacturing sector. They were also well suited to women, since they
required less brawn and more communication skills.

It was during these years, 1974–84, that mothers
rushed into the workplace (an increase of 50 percent),
in order to shore up the family wage, or to survive following divorce. These mothers are members of the
"baby boom" generation; their greatest claims to fame
over previous generations are that there are more of
them and they are the first generation in America to
experience a *lower* standard of living than their parents.
This generation must now spend more than twice as

much (44 percent) of their smaller paycheck for the mortgage payment than families in the early seventies, and, according to a report of Congress's Joint Economic Committee, this "boom" generation spends 30 percent less on clothes, gives 38 percent less to charity, and has 75 percent less savings than their parents.[8] This generation is scrambling frantically to hold on to "the good life."

The women's movement which began in the late sixties was swept along by this gradual but overwhelming change in the economic base. Without realizing it, women supplied an ideology which suited the economy's new need for women workers. The crusade for equal rights both glorified the experience of work and gave women equal responsibility for supporting the family. Men were conveniently relieved of the sole responsibility for supporting the family at a time when it became impossible for them to do so. Meanwhile, the hard-fought right to abortion freed women to hold jobs; a woman with four or five children has little energy left over for the marketplace.

But the concept of equality is a trap. Equal rights does not challenge the structure of the economy or the role of the government. Asking to be treated as men are treated is a fundamentally conservative position that asks for no special support from the government or special consideration from employers for working mothers. America lags behind all industrialized nations and many Third World countries in child care, maternity benefits, and health care for women and children. As the richest nation in the world, we rank an abysmal sixteenth in infant mortality.[9]

Equal rights fits all too snugly into the increasingly conservative climate of opinion of the seventies and eighties which maintains that people should take care of themselves without the help of the government, and that employers, like individuals, should be free to act in their own best interests.

When I and other middle-class women initially embraced the concept of equal rights, we surely had no intention of doing the economy a favor. We saw equal rights as a way of righting all the individual and collective snubs we had suffered from men. We hoped to gain a greater sense of accomplishment and power in the men's world than we believed was possible in the women's world. We had no sense that our small, conditional (conditioned upon acting like men) acceptance into male occupations was in any way connected to the increasing demand for secretaries and waitresses.

Our protracted, exhausting fight for the ERA narrowed our vision and obscured our understanding of the changes that were occurring in women's lives. We failed to see that most women were being marched out to work for low wages with no support for child care or housework, because our eyes were fixed on an ideal that would presumably solve all problems. We paid little attention to the drastic changes in divorce and custody laws, which had immediate punitive effects on women and children.

Expecting everything of the ERA, we did not consider that even if passed it had little to offer. The ERA campaign drained millions of dollars and millions of working hours into the attempt to pass an amendment which would have made little or no change in the fundamental conditions of women's lives. California, the golden progressive state, which passed a state equal-rights amendment in 1964 and has been the leader in sex-discrimination suits, has more poor women, more divorces, and a lower standard of living following divorce than the national average. In California women earn only 58.4 cents to every dollar earned by men.[10]

As frustration with failure to pass an equal-rights constitutional amendment grew through the seventies and the early eighties, the feminist position became increasingly defensive. Women scholars and historians who could deal brilliantly with controversies about the condition of women in history felt obliged to present a rigidly united front regarding the condition of women today.

This defensive strategy was painfully illustrated when Professor Rosalind Rosenberg, a professor of women's history, recently testified for Sears against charges of sex discrimination brought by the Equal Employment Opportunity Commission. Professor Rosenberg claimed that historically "men and women have had different interests, goals and aspirations regarding work . . . Because housework and child care continue to affect the women's labor force participation even today, many women choose jobs that complement their family obligations over jobs that might increase and enhance their earning potential."[11] The EEOC used the testimony of another woman historian, Alice Kessler Harris, who countered that such arguments fall "squarely within a long tradition of employer excuses for and manipulations of women's work experience."

Rosenberg was roundly denounced by the majority of women historians in terms like "betrayal" and "outrageous" not so much for the content of her testimony as for the fact that she testified at all.[12] Not all women historians took this line, however; many agreed with Harvard Professor Catherine Clinton: "Not all truths are going to emerge politically correct. This is a sad epoch in women's history when people can be accused of being disloyal for what they think."[13]

Feminists have sadly become prisoners of their own political rhetoric, and this rhetoric is based on a model of equality which is not suited to the lives of most women. The young women I have known as students, as friends, and, unfortunately, as clients in divorce actions, are unprepared to deal with the reality they did not create and do not understand. Although a characteristic of youth is always to have some unrealistic illusions, today's young women, as the inheritors of the egalitarian revolution, find the gap between their expectations and their everyday lives to be profoundly troubling.

My friend Sheila, whom I have known for ten years, is thirty-eight and unmarried.[14] She has helped support the industry of best-sellers that are feeding on women's confusion about men with such titles as *Smart Women, Foolish Choices, Why Women Choose the Wrong Men,* and *Women Who Love Too Much.* These books all take the position that there are perfectly wonderful men out there waiting and that women like Sheila, for their own unconscious destructive reasons, are passing them by. Sheila would like to believe this, for if the problem is within her she can identify it and cure it. But the problem is not Sheila.

Sheila is not a particularly ambitious or career-oriented woman. If pressed, she would call herself a feminist, but she has minimal political interests. She had expected to work as a commercial artist for a while, then to marry, have children, and continue to work on a free-lance basis. When she left college, her primary goal was a good time. She moved to San Francisco, where she got a job with an advertising agency and shared an apartment with two other young women. Sheila was paid as well as the young men artists in advertising, but that was not enough to afford her an apartment of her own.

At twenty-five Sheila fell in love with Joe. They began to live together almost immediately, partly because it was the accepted mode among their circle of friends, and partly because it was economically advantageous. For five years they kept strict accounts in the most egalitarian fashion. Chores and grocery money were evenly allocated. Although they shared many friends, they also maintained separate lives with other friends and their families. Sexual fidelity was not a requirement, although for the most part they were faithful to each other.

After five years Sheila grew restless and demanded more commitment from Joe. She was ready to have children. Joe said he would think about it, but after a few weeks he left her to live with another woman.

Sheila at first believed she had made a bad choice with Joe, selecting a man who was afraid of commitment and had no interest in family. She spent the next six years looking for a family kind of man, like the father and the uncles she had grown up with. Somehow it seemed that all the men she met were more like Joe, or they were divorced and not eager to go the marriage route again.

Sheila knows she is running a losing race against statistics. According to Harvard and Yale researchers, her chances of marrying after thirty-five are only 5 percent and after forty a depressing one percent.[15] Yet she is still willing to blame herself and not face the fact that men have changed, and that there may not be many men like her father or her uncles anymore.

The egalitarian revolution has created a "new man" who is the main benefactor of the revolution. He is under no obligation to support women, since women can do that for themselves. His position in the corporate or political world no longer requires a family backdrop. A generation ago a divorced or never-married man over thirty-five might have been regarded as unstable or sexually questionable; now he may be looked upon with equanimity or even envy. If a man lives alone (or if he doesn't), it is now appropriate and fashionable that he become a gourmet cook and entertain friends regularly, in the way that wives once did. Takeout easily fills the gap on those evenings home alone. If a man chooses not to live alone, marriage is not the only choice; living-together arrangements offer most of the advantages and none of the responsibilities of marriage and family. If a man does choose to marry, he can, thanks to no-fault divorce laws, easily exit the marriage. Men have been liberated from the yoke of marriage.

In the seventies the number of "free men" surged from 3.5 million at the beginning of the decade to 6.8 million at the end; two thirds of these never married. A survey of these never-marrieds revealed the not-surprising opinion that 70 percent looked negatively upon marriage as "restrictive."[16]

Barbara Ehrenreich, in her provocative book *The Hearts of Men: American Dreams and the Flight from Commitment,* argues that in a purely economic sense women in the twentieth century need men more than men need women. Men opted out of the breadwinner ethic well before the current feminist movement, propelled by a deep dissatisfaction about being the sole wage earner.[17] She claims that feminism arose in the sixties at least in part as a response to the departing male breadwinner. If women must work to support themselves, feminism makes it seem a desirable choice rather than a burden.

This theory is at least partly right; men have opted out of the breadwinner ethic, but not necessarily because of a profound dissatisfaction with this role. At the lower end they have been pushed out of it by a shrinking wage which will not support a family, and at the upper end they have gracefully acquiesced to an egalitarian ethic in which women insist on supporting themselves. When a single man asks a single woman, "What do you do?," it is not merely ice-breaking chatter, but a serious evaluation of the woman's breadwinning capabilities.

Whether the egalitarian message of the current women's movement was the chicken or the egg, it certainly abetted the male flight from the economic and emotional responsibilities of family. Women like Sheila want children, but need the help and support of a husband.

Sheila observed, "I know women who have children on their own, but I'm not ready for that—not yet. I'm afraid I would get sick and not be able to support us. I don't think I could manage."

There is yet another genre of best-selling books telling women what is wrong with them; the message of these books is that their problem is lack of assertiveness, and the need to depend upon men. In a much-praised best-seller, *The Cinderella Complex*, the author, Colette Dowling, maintains that women suffer from a fatal dependency on men, which stifles their creativity and independent thinking. Using her own life as an example, she relates that after many desperate years as a single parent, trying to support three children on a writer's uncertain income, she met a man with whom she set up housekeeping in the country. She describes the domestic bliss of decorating and gardening that she claims quickly destroyed her creativity and rendered her less than self-supporting. She berates herself for this sluggishness, and her partner berates her for not bringing home the bacon.[18]

From this author's point of view the slightest bow to dependency turns a woman into a domestic slug, totally extinguishing her creative self. But in fact this woman author carried a substantial burden for many years and finally got some support and a little breathing space. Making curtains for a few months did not destroy her talent or her career. A boost of economic and domestic support allowed her to climb out of a bare-survival mode and do more interesting things—such as writing a best-selling book.

Dependence has become one of the blackest buzz words of the egalitarian crusade, evoking images of infantilized women who live on the scraps from their husbands' lives. But a woman with children needs to depend upon others to help her with the serious and difficult business of raising them. And she has the right to expect it—from a husband, from an ex-husband, or from a man who chooses to live with her and her children. In a distortion of the ideal of independence, women have assumed complete responsibility not only for themselves but for their children as well.

It makes sense for women who have children, or who want children, to seek a familial model for raising them. In a family, the individual does not always come first, and the economic and work arrangements are not always scrupulously equal. It is, however, a community in which the members can mutually depend upon each other.

My friend Myra was a thorough feminist of the seventies who placed career above all and would have scorned the dependent traits of a Cinderella. Myra aspired to be a judge. When she met fellow law student Jim, who planned to become a politician, she felt confident that they could establish an egalitarian partnership with mutually compatible career goals.

Myra and Jim were twenty-four when they married in 1975. They discussed their career aspirations endlessly, talked vaguely about having children once their careers were in place, and agreed to share domestic responsibilities equally.

Following law school they veered slightly from their dreams. Jim got an offer from a big law firm which he couldn't resist, rationalizing that there was plenty of time for politics. Myra took a job as a public defender which she felt was a good route toward an eventual judgeship. Their household routine was still fairly egalitarian, but with more money they ate out frequently— every night in busy times. Both had hectic schedules, but as a new associate Jim was expected to put in sixty to seventy hours each week.

As she neared thirty Myra decided it was time to have a child. She planned to take off three months from her job as public defender, the maximum allowed by the law of her state (unpaid sick leave), and find live-in help.

"I was unprepared for how absolutely absorbing and exhausting a baby is," recalled Myra, "and child care was a nightmare." Myra and Jim had enough money to afford live-in help, but the women she hired proved unreliable and she was forced to change help three times in the baby's first year. Myra told Jim he would have to help more during these constant child-care crises or she would lose her job, and Jim pointed out that he would have to give up a job which paid twice as much as hers if he cut down his hours to accommodate the baby.

Myra quit her job as a public defender and felt increasingly resentful toward Jim. He was able to pursue his dreams and she was not. Part-time jobs in law were scarce and unrewarding. The tension between them worsened, and finally it was Myra who left Jim. "At the time I felt I couldn't live with a part-time husband who had no concern for my needs," she says.

The judge at the divorce trial awarded Myra no spousal support, noting that as a professional woman she could certainly take care of herself. This was in keeping with the spirit and letter of the California no-fault divorce laws. He ordered $250 per month child support. Myra now had no choice but to work full time in order to support herself and Tod, now four. She found an appropriate nursery-school/day-care arrangement, but she had to pick up the child by five-thirty. She finally found a law job that never required late hours or trial appearances and allowed her to miss work when her child was sick. "I'm assisting a personal-injury lawyer—medical records, interrogatories, that sort of thing. It's boring and I don't get paid much more than the legal secretary, but it's all I can handle."

Jim is now a partner, but still works long hours. Even though he has joint custody he finds time to take Tod only on occasional weekends or evenings, often making the arrangement at the last minute. "I don't hate Jim anymore, I just envy him, he's doing so well, and I can hardly make it through the month."

Myra's story is not the tragedy of a woman who is forced into seeking public assistance when her husband of twenty-five years leaves her for a new life. Myra will not be registered among the "official poor," but her story is something of a modern tragedy nonetheless. There are no human villains in her story. Jim would not share the child care equally, but it is a fact that in the very demanding profession of law an attorney who offers less than full time plus commitment must accept poorly paid, tedious work. Is the solution for both partners to work part time and threaten economic security for the family? Perhaps one of the only professions which allows such flexible scheduling is the university world, and it is not surprising that most suggestions for egalitarian child care come from that quarter.

Myra is the victim of the climate of egalitarian expectations. She was encouraged to live to work, to seek a high-status job in a male profession. But, like most male professions, it made no allowances for family obligations. Myra was not prepared for the relentless way in which motherhood thwarted her ambition and changed the nature of her apparently egalitarian marriage. As a modern couple Myra and Jim chose divorce as a solution to the tension between them.

Myra is a bitter woman. She feels that she is a failure. It is true that in ten years or so the yoke of her single parenthood will be lifted, but law is not the sort of profession that allows you to drop in and out of the race. There are too few jobs and too many young energetic competitors.

In the Academy Award–winning film *Kramer versus Kramer,* Joanna Kramer also feels thwarted by the burden of motherhood and marriage and solves the problem by leaving both her husband and her child. The audience has a difficult time with this character: she expresses the modern need for egalitarian fulfillment portrayed with quiet agony by actress Meryl Streep, but she also abandons her child, an act which society is not willing to condone. A convincing subtheme of the story is that when the father, played by Dustin Hoffman, is forced into the role of single parent, he cannot hold on to his high-powered, demanding job in advertising and is forced to take a less well-paid inferior position.

The conflict between primary caretaker and career is sharply etched in this drama, which is ultimately resolved (following a custody trial which does not represent modern law) when Streep chooses career over motherhood. This choice is confused in the film by the scene-stealing performances of Hoffman as the modern nuturing father who will sacrifice career for fatherhood.

Although the film accurately hits a modern nerve in its representation of the conflict of parenthood and career, its resolution does not. In life outside the movie world the mother, like Myra, will most often be the one to make the career sacrifice, with or without divorce. Even with relaxed custody laws in most states, it is a rare occurrence for a man to seek physical custody when there is a competent mother. Contrary to the Dustin Hoffman single-father image, the number of single-father-headed households, according to demographer Andrew Hacker, actually declined in the seventies.[19] It is rare for a competent mother to voluntarily give up the custody of children under age thirteen.

The conflict between the familial model of dependence and the autonomous model of independence is not a new experience for American women. Carl Degler, in his ground-breaking work *At Odds: Women and Family in America from the Revolution to the Present,* claims that "women and the family, in truth, have been in enduring tension for at least two centuries."[20] This tension has not been static, it has grown steadily and is now at a breaking point. Degler asserts: "Many women today find the realization of themselves as persons impossible to achieve within a family situation. Yet most women still consider a family relationship as more important to them than the realization of their own individuality."[21]

In all but recent times a relief from the tension created by women's conflicting needs for autonomy and dependence were sought by the great majority of feminists in a manner which did not directly threaten the family. Only a few nineteenth-century feminists urged equality with men in the family; these included Elizabeth Cady Stanton, who declared, "When woman is man's equal the marriage relationship cannot stand on the basis it is today. . . . Let us remember that womanhood is the great fact, wifehood and motherhood its incidents." But even Stanton never argued that women should cease to be the primary child-rearers.[22]

A flexible concept of women's rights, however, rather than a strict concept of equality, was the focus of most organized women's activities in the nineteenth century and the first half of the twentieth. Women's rights included new laws or changes in the old laws which would improve the lives of women but would not necessarily require complete equality with men; in fact, the laws these women promoted, in particular the laws to protect women from unsafe factory conditions, were often protective rather than egalitarian.

By the end of the nineteenth century, thanks to women's-rights pressure at the state level, most states had substantially modified the common-law doctrine of *femme couverte* under which wives had been chattels of their husbands, with no direct legal control over their own earnings, children, or property, unless a premarital agreement had been negotiated and their property placed in trust. (That trust was usually controlled by a male relative.) New laws gave wives control over their inherited property and their earnings. Women were granted the chance of custody in the rare event of divorce; previously the children had always been granted to the father.[23] But women's-rights reformers did not attempt to remove the obligation of men to support their families, and they strongly supported the family unit as the essential core of society.

At the beginning of the twentieth century progressive women reformers like Jane Addams at Hull House and Lilian Wald at Henry Street, the two most famous women settlement workers, joined forces with the Women's Trade Union League and the Consumers' League to fight for women, children, and the home. Almost all women's-rights reformers were educated middle-class women, but many devoted their entire energy to becoming advocates for poor women, who were often immigrants, and their children. They were instrumental in founding the Children's Bureau, and in the drafting of child-labor laws. The settlement houses provided special services for poor women, including visiting-nurse services and nurseries and kindergartens for working mothers.[24]

In the workplace these reformers focused on protective state legislation for women which included maximum-hour and minimum-wage laws for women and special safety requirements. They also restricted the occupations in which a woman could work; for example, selling liquor or driving taxis was considered inappropriate for women in some states. These laws are currently criticized as restricting women from men's jobs, but at the time many of them radically attacked the horrors of working conditions in many factories and sometimes made the conditions safer for men as well. The courts were unwilling to grant such protection to men, arguing that it interfered with "freedom of contract," but were willing to grant it to women because of their special position as mothers or potential mothers.[25]

As the century wore on, the battle for women's rights narrowed in focus and expanded in support. Suffrage became the single panacea by which women would change all that was wrong with society; but suffrage was not intended to change the family, rather to protect it. Motherhood was looked upon with the highest reverence, attributing to it a kind of mystical moral superiority. "Women are the mothers of the race, and as such are admittedly more concerned than anyone else with all that goes to protect life," declared a young feminist lawyer, Inez Milholland, as she led a New York City suffrage parade.[26] It was believed that because of their superior moral sense women would wield the vote to stop corruption and vice, prevent wars, and end all discrimination against women.[27]

The suffrage achieved in 1920 accomplished very little except the collapse of an impressive political machine. There are nearly as many theorists as there are theories to explain why it proved to be such a paper tiger. A popular theory, put forth by suffrage historian William O'Neill in his book *Everyone Was Brave*, argues that suffrage was always a blind alley, since it left the family sacrosanct. The only way that equality between the sexes could be achieved, he declared, would be by a revolution in domestic life.[28]

The current crop of feminists sprouted in the late sixties in the wake of the black civil-rights movement and took on that revolution in domestic life. Their inspiration for a rejection of women's rights in favor of equal rights came directly from the rhetoric of black civil rights.

American women in the nineteenth and twentieth centuries have identified their struggle with that of blacks. This has always been a philosophical rather than a practical political alliance. In the nineteenth century women split off from the antislavery movement to found their own Women's Rights Convention in 1848 when male antislavery activists made it clear that they were not going to give women's rights equal attention. In 1967 they were spurned again when black activist Stokely Carmichael bluntly stated, "The position of women in our movement should be prone,"[29] thus aborting a potential alliance and once again launching women into their own movement.

The black struggle in the nineteenth century (carried on largely by white men) was first for freedom from slavery and then for specific rights before the law, including suffrage. In the recent twentieth century, beginning in the late fifties, the focus changed sharply, and the struggle became a battle to erase race as a consideration in all areas of life. In this country

the strategy for ending racism has not been the aboli-
tion of private property as the barrier to equality, as
it has been with communism; instead it has been the
right to compete for power with white males in the
marketplace. This is in keeping with the distinctly
American ethic of "rugged individualism." But it meant
that white men, rather than abstract capitalists or the
bourgeoisie, were considered the oppressors.

Identifying with the contemporary black struggle for
equality was a mistake for women. By analogy with the
black movement, many feminists placed all men in the
role of the oppressors, and they encouraged abusive
attacks on men in the early part of the current wom-
en's movement from which the movement has not yet
recovered. If "Whitey" was a pig, then men were pigs.
For a time in the early seventies, groups like SCUM,
or Society to Cut Up Men, titillated the media. For
some women, cohabiting with the enemy became an
act of political treason, as it was for the extreme black
separatists. For black men this may have been an effective political tool; for women it was a direct assault on
the men who had been their partners in the family unit.

As racial differences became suspect, so, too, gender
differences. Women attacked any reference to biological differences between men and women as fiercely as
blacks attacked allegations of biological racial differences. Socialization, not biology, accounted for the
accepted roles of women as nurturers and men as
aggressors.

Male and female differences regarding sexuality inevitably came under attack, serving as the catalyst to
the sexual revolution which shattered traditional patterns of courtship and marriage. Women were encouraged to reverse the hold of socialization and become
sexual aggressors. Marriage was seen as patriarchal and
controlling, living together as egalitarian and liberating.

Children became problematical, since they shifted the egalitarian balance. For the first time it became an accepted and even applauded choice for women to turn down motherhood.

But it was identification with the black drive to grab power from white men in the marketplace that has proved most troublesome for women. At the same time that women were pulled into the marketplace in great numbers, they chose a competitive strategy which was ill-suited for the reality of their lives. By the mid-seventies the marketplace had become the focus of the egalitarian crusade, and it has remained so. Title VII of the Civil Rights Act of 1964, which forbids discrimination in employment based on race and sex, was drafted for *blacks* to compete with white males in the marketplace. It originally prohibited discrimination based specifically on race, *not* sex. By a last-minute lobbying sleight-of-hand, sex was included in the bill.

This law, which has become the major weapon in women's battle for equality at work, was designed for black men, not for women. The great majority of women are clustered in female occupations like teaching, nursing, and data processing, where there are few, if any, white males with whom to achieve equality. In the male-dominated echelons of law, medicine, and top management, the law allows women to compete with men on men's terms. For women with children this means running as a handicapped racer.

A bill written for the needs of working women would not have stressed equal competition, but would address the issues of government-subsidized child care, paid maternity leaves, a higher minimum wage (since 65 percent of all minimum-wage workers are women), medical care and pension rights for part-time workers, affirmative action, and reentry rights. It would also require some form of pay equity between male-dominated occupations and female-dominated occupations. Instead, women have trapped themselves into a competitive model that leaves no room for the special needs of women who are the primary child-rearers.

Many feminists claim that the solution to the problems of working mothers is not government involvement, but an egalitarian sharing of the child-care and domestic responsibilities between father and mother. Aside from the fact that many working women have no husband at home to share with, it is a truth that in all industrialized countries, including enlightened Sweden, women who work still bear the great majority of child-care responsibilities.

The basic problem is that children need adult supervision twenty-four hours a day until they are themselves nearly adult. Even with the most egalitarian sharing between partners there is still a need for outside help. An economy that requires the labor of women in the marketplace must pay for the consequences of taking that labor from the home.

Title VII not only does not ask for support for working mothers but was used by some feminists to *strike down* a California law which would provide a four-month unpaid maternity leave, on the grounds that it does not treat *men* equally.

Lillian Garland took an *unpaid* pregnancy leave from her job as a receptionist with California Federal Savings and Loan in Los Angeles in 1982. Under a 1978 California law, the savings-and-loan institution was obliged to give her back her old job. Cal Fed challenged the law on the grounds that it discriminated against men and therefore was in conflict with the equal treatment mandated by Title VII. The federal district court agreed with this logic and threw out the maternity-leave law.

This case, California Federal Savings and Loan Association v. Guerra,[30] which eventually reached the Supreme Court, clearly illustrates the paradoxical trap of strict egalitarian logic. Instead of rallying to the defense of maternity leaves, women, particularly women lawyers, divided on the issue, many claiming that indeed women had to be treated equally and should demand no special privileges. The National Organization for Women (NOW) and the National Women's Political Caucus (NWPC), the two most powerful feminist groups, joined in filing a friend-of-the-court brief *supporting* the savings-and-loan challenge to overturn the law. They argued that Title VII mandates that pregnant women must be treated just the same as temporarily disabled men. (In California the job would not be held for four months for a disabled man.)[31]

The majority (six to three) of the Supreme Court disagreed with the feminists. They wrestled with the fundamental conflict between equal treatment and preferential treatment by comparing maternity leaves with affirmative action and came up with the logic, as expressed by Justice John Paul Stevens, that "preferential treatment of the disadvantaged class is only permissible so long as it is consistent with accomplishing the goals that Congress intended Title VII to achieve."[32] California and other states are now free to pass laws which will give preferential treatment to pregnant workers.

The pregnancy issue is a serious snare in the skein of egalitarian logic. It has become popular in feminist circles and in Congress to advocate an *unpaid* parental leave which either partner can take. This egalitarian solution cleverly avoids the obvious truth that childbirth is not an equal situation. It is the woman who gives birth, and it is the woman who needs the leave in order to maintain her health before childbirth and to regain her strength following delivery. For many women following a difficult birth this can be weeks or months. How many families can survive if both bread-winners bring home far less than full pay? Surely the mother deserves first priority in taking time off. A pa-rental leave will work only if at least one parent still receives full pay, otherwise it is simply egalitarian window-dressing. This has been the experience of in-stitutions that already offer paternity leaves. The New York City Board of Education, which has offered pater-nity leaves since 1973, regularly grants about two thou-sand leaves each year to mothers and four or five leaves to fathers.[33]

This maternity-leave case is the latest bout in the old and painful conflict between a women's-rights and an equal-rights strategy. When Alice Paul's Woman's Party first introduced the Equal Rights Amendment in Con-gress, in 1926, the great majority of women who had campaigned for and successfully won suffrage in 1920 considered it a betrayal of their ideals. Suffrage leaders, including Carrie Chapman Catt, Florence Kelley, and Jane Addams, were outraged. They claimed it would strike down the much-needed legislation which pro-tected women from ghastly working conditions in fac-tories. Obtaining this protective legislation had been a lifelong struggle for many of these women. They believed that women needed special consideration be-cause of their role as mothers.[34] Fifty years later, inspired by the rhetoric of civil rights and encouraged by a marketplace that courts them, the great majority of feminists now believe that women should be treated as individuals, not as a sex—that free and open com-petition with men in the marketplace is the goal.

A competitive model which asks for no special favors may be good for business, but it is bad for women with children. And in spite of its devaluation by the current feminist wave, motherhood seems in no danger of

dying out. It is marriage and the traditional family that
are on the critical list. Although the number of children
that an individual woman bears has decreased over the
last one hundred years, the proportion of women giving
birth to a single child or no child at all has remained
fairly stable.[35] Without venturing into the turbulent
waters surrounding biological drive, it appears that
women clearly opt for motherhood, since at this time
in history it is for the most part a matter of personal
choice.

This is a critical juncture in the history of women in
America. For the first time the great majority of *married* women are working outside the home (even 48
percent with children less than one year old[36]), and for
the first time the divorce rate nearly equals the marriage rate. The prerogatives of our economy indicate
that women do not have the choice to return to the
home, and for increasing numbers there is no traditional
home there to return to. More than at any time in
history women need help from men, from each other,
and from the government, to bear their double burden
of work and family.[37]

It is time for some hard rethinking and reevaluation
of the direction of the women's movement. A return to
the flexible, pragmatic concept of women's rights, rather
than the rigid ideology of equal rights, is in order. This
will require a change of heart as well as a change of
mind. The idea of women's rights recognizes and promotes the role of motherhood and family in the lives
of women, equal rights does not.

Somehow, the family, which is important to all men
and women who have spent time in one, has become
the private reserve of the right end of the political
spectrum. Surely, the fate of children and marriage can
pull together women of all political persuasions to
engage in a free discussion which may bring down the

stone walls of ideological certainty. Women on the left, the right and the middle are all affected by the change in the economic base which has sent them out of the home to help make ends meet. This strain on family life cuts across all political differences.

The tradition of women's rights also embraces poor women who cannot fight for themselves. Between 1970 and 1985 the numbers of families living below the poverty line jumped by a staggering 36 percent. The vast majority of these "new poor" are women and children. Most women today who are pushed into the job market at the low end, or who find themselves the victims of divorce, do not have the skills or the organization to pull themselves up. They need, but are not getting, the attention and support of well-organized middle-class women.

The concept of equality need not be abandoned entirely, but should be used as only one weapon in a larger arsenal, and it must be restricted to those situations where it will help rather than hinder women. Equality in education for young women without family responsibilities makes sense. But equal opportunity in jobs is useful only in limited situations, and must be combined with a wide range of other strategies.

Women's rights can be adapted to meet the evolving needs of women. The following chapters will not just raise questions but will suggest practical strategies and solutions for a rejuvenated women's-rights movement. They will focus on family law and conditions in the workplace, the areas of acute crisis in women's lives today.

Radical changes in the structure of marriage and in divorce procedures will be proposed to counter the morally bankrupt and punitive effects of no-fault divorce on women with children and older displaced homemakers. Suggestions to counter the popular but pernicious egalitarian trend toward judicially imposed joint custody will be offered. "Family law" is presented as a broad program which supports healthy families, rather than as a procedure for picking up the pieces after a family collapses.

Women in the workplace will be separated and examined in four categories: women who live to work (these are the women who are tackling male-dominated professions); women who work to live (these are the majority of women who are flooding into female occupations); women who work part time or casually; and reentry and older women. Most analyses of the problems of working women lump all women into a single image: they are represented either as Rosie the Riveter or as Lady Lawyer marching with briefcase to trial. In fact working women in each of these groups experience very different problems which require very different solutions.

The American workplace is complex; for example, two out of five workers are employed by government in some form. The so-called free market is already studded with special-preference pockets created by unions, licenses, tenure systems, and the minimum wage. Practical suggestions will be offered to improve the lot of each category of women working within this complexity. Unionism will be examined anew, and the modern women's branches of old male professional organizations will be looked to for grass-roots changes in working conditions and for developing new career paths. Concrete suggestions regarding day care, the nightmare which plagues most working women, will be offered.

The tension between the egalitarian Title VII and the preferential treatment offered by affirmative action and comparable worth will be closely examined. The failure of the male competitive model is admitted with comparable worth, which recognizes that most women, for good and practical reasons, are not going to compete directly with men and will remain in female-dominated occupations.

Equality is a trap for women. Over the past twenty years the condition of women has seriously worsened, not improved. A new vision must be developed to deal with women's increasing poverty, with their overload of work, with the breakdown of their families. Updating a durable concept, women's rights, to deal with the new problems of modern women in a changing economy is the most effective way of dealing with this crisis.

2

NO-FAULT DIVORCE: THE EGALITARIAN TRIUMPH

Divorce has become the number-one social and economic problem for women and children. The divorce rate exploded in the seventies, with nearly one out of two marriages ending in the courts. The victims of this explosion are mothers and their children. One quarter of *all* children now live in single-parent households; the single parent is the mother nine times out of ten.[1] Most of these single-parent households are the consequence of divorce. There has been a good deal of optimistic talk about the evolution of the family, or the creation of the "new family." This "new family," however, is most often a woman alone with children, trying to hold on against the slide into poverty. Fifty percent of these mothers have lost the battle and are below the official poverty line.[2]

No-fault divorce, which swept through nearly all the states in the seventies, is not the only cause of the divorce revolution, but it removed the moral and economic sting from a previously forbidding legal procedure and allowed millions of people to do what until then was for them the unthinkable. Making divorce easier has been an economic disaster for women and children.

No-fault is more than just a legal transformation, it is a state of mind. One of the most difficult experiences for me during my own no-fault divorce was that everyone, including my parents, made careful remarks such as "Couples grow apart" or "These things happen nowadays." Not a whisper of blame was placed or any hint of outrage expressed about the breaking up of a family. No one said it was a terrible thing to happen to a family, but it was.

In the current climate of opinion, no-fault has come to mean no responsibility. The noble concept of equality has soured into the distorted notion that both parties are equally responsible and therefore no one is responsible when a family breaks up. What began as an attempt to take moral issues out of the courtroom has resulted in the elimination of the moral issue.

"You can't legislate morality," was the angry conservative response to the comprehensive civil-rights laws which integrated schools, public accommodations, housing, and the workplace in the sixties. But this country, which does not sponsor a national church, and where families are mobile and generations far-flung, depends on its laws to set the moral climate. Public opinion has dutifully followed the lead set by the de-legislation of morality from divorce. Even the generations reared in the firm faith that divorce was quasi-criminal have been reeducated. One fourth of all divorces are now among people married more than fifteen years. Twenty-five years ago this figure was 4 percent.[3]

State legislatures rushed to enact no-fault divorce after California introduced the concept in 1969. Forty-nine out of the fifty states now boast some form of no-fault.[4] In some states one disgruntled party may merely complain that the marriage has reached a point of "irretrievable breakdown," no matter what the reality, or the needs or wishes of the other party. In other states "incompatibility" or "irreconcilable differences" must be demonstrated if one party objects, but it is considered sufficient proof if one partner chooses to walk out and live separately. In some of the more conservative states, living separate and apart for a period of time (from six months to three years) is the only ground for divorce.[5] The result is that in every state but one, either the husband or the wife can leave a marriage at will.

The egalitarian ideal behind no-fault is to treat the marital partners as equal autonomous adults with the ability to make decisions without the intrusion of the courts, thereby avoiding messy court battles. No-fault was widely favored by feminists and progressive groups as a way of promoting individual freedom. The concept worked hand in glove with women's search for equality through the rejection of the patriarchal family, and with men's moving out of their role as protector and breadwinner. It also fit nicely with the narcissism of the seventies, when everyone seemed to be intently engaged in the search for self.

The rationale behind the old divorce laws was protection rather than equality. It was generally accepted that the state had a legitimate role in protecting the family from frivolous or immoral conduct by one of the partners. If one party deserted or committed adultery, he or she would be severely punished in the property-settlement and spousal-support arrangements. This punishment extended to public opinion well beyond the family circle. In recent history, 1964, public opinion turned against the nomination of Nelson A. Rockefeller for President when he left his wife of many years for another woman.

Under the old laws, if one partner merely wanted out and neither party had committed a grievous offense, he or she would have to strike some sort of private bargain for freedom or stay in the marriage. By today's lights these ideas seem archaically vengeful and an unacceptable restraint on individual freedom, but they were protective of the family unit. Divorce could not be an option of an individual whim.

The momentum in current law is to extend the no-fault concept beyond grounds for divorce to property settlements and continuing support. As a logical extension of the policy that each party has an equal right to renounce the marriage at any point for any reason, or no reason at all, the law in most states dictates that each party has a right to the property accumulated during the marriage, no questions asked. This takes the economic as well as the moral sting out of leaving a marriage. In many cases this allows an oppressed wife to walk away from an oppressive husband without fear that she will lose all property rights, but it also allows a philandering husband (or wife) to leave with impunity. Nineteen states lead this trend by expressly excluding marital fault from consideration in distributing property, while thirteen states are silent on this issue. Alimony awards are increasingly no-fault oriented; most states refuse to consider fault when determining support.[6]

In some community-property states like California, the post–no-fault knife slices cleanly down the middle, with no special consideration for fault or for family circumstances; the law clearly instructs the court to divide the assets and liabilities equally.[7] This sounds good, but since the family home is the only major asset for most families, an equal split requires that it be sold and the assets divided. This legal action forces women and children, who remain with their mothers in 90 percent of divorced families,[8] into inferior housing in inferior neighborhoods.

Most other states have adopted a theory of equitable distribution of property following no-fault, which allows the judge a good deal of discretion. Equity in the courts means fairness, not equality. It allows taking into account special circumstances such as minor children, length of marriage, ability to support, and, in some states, fault. This is certainly the fairest approach, but the written guidelines vary from state to state, and in some states they are entirely absent. This can lead to wildly varying decisions within a state and huge differences in the norm between states. Generally, however, women with children keep the family home.

It is with spousal support (alimony) and child support that women and children have been most damaged by the deadly combination of no-fault divorce and egalitarian attitudes. Although the divorce laws in the individual states do not insist upon it, judges have taken the position that women with children can support themselves as well as men can support themselves. It is as if every time the media announces that a woman has been appointed to a judgeship or a high corporate position thousands of women lose spousal support. Feminists complain that judges are punishing women for women's liberation. In fact judges are receiving the message that feminists are sending: they want to be given a chance to compete with men in the marketplace; they do not want to be taken care of and made dependent.

There is a relentless trend toward no alimony at all or short-term alimony for "rehabilitative" purposes, as opposed to the long-term or lifelong alimony in pre–no-fault days. Most states bar fault as a consideration in making any award. Some states specify the uppermost length of alimony, usually one or two years, and a few states severely restrict the conditions under which it may be granted at all. Indiana, for instance, allows alimony only for a "physically or mentally handicapped spouse."[9] The U.S. Census data shows that of the 17 million divorced women in this country, 85 percent received no alimony at all.

The severe cutback in alimony has not been offset by an increase in child support. In fact, child-support awards have dropped drastically in recent years. Between 1978 and 1981, child-support awards nationally dropped 16 percent, with inflation taken into account. They took another 12.4 percent dive between 1983 and 1985, for a total decrease of 28.4 percent.[10] When child support is collected (less than 50 percent of the time), it pays for far less than half the cost of raising the child. (Custody and child support will be thoroughly examined in Chapter Three.)

No-fault has left unprotected both the young woman who must now support both herself and her family, and the older woman who has few skills with which to support herself.

One of my first divorce clients, we'll call her Louise Butler, was sixty years old and was severely injured in an auto accident which left her with limited movement in one arm and one leg. She required continuing therapy and faced the dismal prospect of more operations.

Louise was married twenty-five years ago with the legal and social promise that she would raise the children and provide a good home while her husband would support and protect her for life. Her husband, a highly paid professional, broke the promise by leaving her for another woman.

I approached her husband's attorney with a reasonable offer for spousal support based on the fact that she could not work and would require continuing expensive medical treatment. The attorney replied that he would not consider spousal support, since there would be significant assets from the sale of the house and she would have a share of her husband's retirement (ten years hence). At first I was shocked, but after reviewing the very confused post–no-fault decisions in California at that point, I feared he had some law to stand on.

Since the assets from the house would soon be spent on medical care (she would, of course, lose her husband's medical insurance), Louise could easily slip into destitution, while her husband would continue to live on his high income. We decided to take the case to court. Only a small percentage of divorce cases are actually litigated, because the cost of doing so is often greater than the amount in question.

Louise was lucky. The virtual extermination of long-term spousal support for older women in long marriages had caused such grievous hardship for thousands of women that the California legislature was compelled to patch a Band-Aid on the system. Before Louise's case came to trial in 1981 the legislature amended the law to specifically direct the judge to consider "the earning capacity of each spouse, taking into account the extent to which the supported spouse's present and future earning capacity is impaired by periods of unemployment that were incurred during the marriage to permit the supported spouse to devote time to domestic duties.[11] This law quickly became popularly known as the "Displaced Homemakers' Relief Act."

The Displaced Homemakers' Relief Act saved Louise

from destitution. The judge awarded her modest spousal support which will allow her to live on the good edge of the poverty line. But in our crazy-quilt state-by-state system, most displaced homemakers are not so "lucky." They are usually given a short period of support in which to find employment. Those who do find employment find it at the bottom of the wage scale. Those who do not find employment are thrown onto their own resources, since, if their children are grown, they are often not eligible for public assistance.

Edith Curtis, following the abrupt end of a thirty-year marriage to a college professor, argued before the Idaho Supreme Court that she should be considered for unemployment insurance, since she had helped her husband's career, performing the duties of faculty wife, and that she had been relieved of that job. The only job she could find to replace it was as a part-time cashier at a fast-food restaurant at minimum wage. Her thirty-year-old English degree was useless. She was reduced to living in a one-room cabin without plumbing and to eating church giveaway food. The court dismissed her case as frivolous.[12]

In the fifty-plus generation, no-fault divorce is having a widespread devastating effect. Marriages that survived the seven-year itch, launched the children, and welcomed the grandchildren are collapsing almost as fast as younger marriages. Older divorced women have grown so numerous that they have been grouped generically as "displaced homemakers." These are women who have worked outside the home for a short time or not at all and have dedicated the best years of their lives to supporting their husbands and children. They have developed domestic skills which are not valued by the marketplace, and have lost the confidence they had as attractive young women.

My client, Louise, was "lucky" because she lived in a

state which recognized her right to a share in her husband's pension. Many women are not so lucky. The divorce explosion has forced public attention to the Pandora's box of conflicting and confused laws regarding a divorced spouse's interest in the former spouse's pension. (Most often, but not always, this is the nonpensioned wife's interest in her former husband's pension.) For older women this is often the chief asset upon which they were planning their survival in old age.

Individual states vary greatly in how they treat a pension upon divorce. Some see it as community property to be apportioned based on the length of the community. States which support equitable division often, but not always, look at the pension as one of the assets to be considered upon divorce. The trend is certainly toward considering pensions as a factor in a property settlement, but there are still states that flatly refuse to recognize any interest in a pension if it is not already vested—i.e., has a current cash-out value. If Louise had lived in Colorado, for instance, she would have received nothing from her husband's pension plan, since it had no cash value until he reached sixty-five.[13]

The confusion surrounding alimony and pension plans indicates that our legal and social system is not prepared to expect divorce for older women; it is much better prepared for widowhood. Although it is impossible to compare the personal pain experienced from the death of a spouse with the pain of divorce, an economic comparison can be made. If Louise's husband had died, rather than left her, his employee benefit package would have given her twice his annual salary in life insurance (with no contribution on his part), a continuation of medical insurance, and full survivor pension benefits when she reached age sixty-two. She would, of course, have full ownership of the house and their other assets. There was also a substantial term life-insurance policy of which she was the beneficiary. As a divorced wife she lost all these benefits. It is ironic that the same husband who planned carefully for his wife in the event of his death was quite prepared to leave her with nothing when he divorced her.

Socially she would have fared better as well. Relatives and friends would have offered her solid support during her period of grief. She would not have felt compelled to move from the community, as she did, in order to avoid meeting her ex-husband and his new love. Friends would not have to choose sides; a certain social continuity could be maintained. Even in our enlightened times, her social status would be less ambiguous and less threatening as a widow than as a divorcee. Our culture has had much more experience with widows than it has had with divorcees.

On the other end of the divorce spectrum, the young woman with children has not been rescued by a Single Parent Relief Act in California or anywhere else. In California, where the effects of no-fault have been longest observed, only 13 percent of mothers with preschool children were awarded spousal support following the enactment of the new no-fault divorce law in 1970, compared with 20 percent in 1968, and the awards were much smaller. The child-support awards were rarely enough to cover half the costs of raising the children.[14]

Today's young women, filled with egalitarian expectations, never expect to find themselves in the exhausting and impoverished state of single parenthood, but they do in tragically large numbers.

My client Mary Ludden met Jim Smith in 1968 at a small private Catholic college near San Francisco when they were both undergraduates.[15] As was common for their generation, they married upon graduation, in 1970. Mary was not aware that no-fault was introduced in

California that year but, as with most brides, divorce
law would not have interested her.

A prudent young couple, Mary and Jim both worked
for two years, he as an insurance salesman, she as an assistant librarian at their college, where she had begun
working as a student. They saved enough money to
make a down payment on a modest $35,000 home and
to create a small nest egg for law school for Jim. Jim entered law school in 1972, continuing to work part time
as a sales clerk in a liquor store. Mary continued to
work in the library, and their first child, Jill, was born
in 1974. Mary took a six-month maternity leave and
then returned to work, leaving Jill in a home-care arrangement.

In 1975 Jim passed the California bar and was offered
a beginning associate's job. They thought their tough
financial times were over, and their second child, Ar-
thur, was born in 1976. This time Mary did not return
to work. After a couple of years as an associate Jim
grew restless. He decided that he wanted to set up his
own practice and felt that Los Angeles would provide
better opportunities. Mary was reluctant to leave family and friends, but finally agreed. Jim went to Los Angeles to scout out law offices, and two days later Mary
received a long letter in which Jim explained that he
had married too young and he needed to "find himself."
She next heard from him when she was served with a
notice that he had filed for divorce.

Following the letter of the law, the Smiths' property
and debts were equally divided. Fortunately, there were
no debts, but their assets included the house, which had
inflated in the California real-estate market to a value
of $70,000, and a small car. Jim claimed he needed his
half immediately in order to set up a practice, so the
court ordered the house sold. The sale yielded a profit

of $35,000, but after real-estate-broker and divorce-attorney fees Mary's half was only $12,000. The court then ordered $300 in monthly child support but no spousal support, since the community property assets were considered "substantial" and Jim could claim a negative cash flow from his fledgling practice. Mary got the five-year-old car.

The major asset of their marriage was Jim's professional training, to which Mary had contributed by working to support him for many years. Those years of schooling cost a great deal in terms of the loss of Jim's wages that might have gone into the bank or other assets which could have been divided on divorce. Jim retained all the benefits of the law degree which will give him a lifelong advantage in earning money. Mary got nothing for her efforts.

This issue of professional training to which one spouse has contributed by helping support the other (usually wife putting husband through school) has been hotly litigated in California and elsewhere. Mary, like most wives, did not support Jim as a gift to her husband. She fully expected to join in the economic benefits of her sacrifice. The bargain, though unwritten, was clearly understood by both husband and wife.

The nation, or at least the nation of family-law attorneys and their clients, held their breaths for two years while Sullivan v. Sullivan waited before the California Supreme Court, the trailblazer in family-law issues. In this case Janet Sullivan had worked for many years to put her husband, Mark, through medical school. When they divorced, she wanted a continuing share of his income as compensation. The result was a sore disappointment for women in this position. The legislature preempted a Supreme Court decision by passing legislation, widely known in the legal community as the "Mark and Janet Sullivan Memorial Statute," which dictated that the complaining spouse could ask only for "community contributions to education or training of a party that substantially enhances the earning capacity of the party" plus interest, effective January 1, 1985[16] (too late for Mary). It is unclear exactly what "community contributions" might mean. Probably it will be interpreted as the cost of tuition but not future earnings.

After the divorce, Mary Ludden (she took back her maiden name) returned to work at the library, the only job she could find with her skills, and for her a comforting, familiar environment. She put both her children (now ages two and four) into home care, at a cost of $500 per month. With high interest rates and a low salary, she could not afford a condominium and was forced to pay $500 for a small two-bedroom apartment twenty-five miles from her job; this was $300 more per month than her home-mortgage payments had been. Her original monthly budget looked like this:

INCOME	EXPENSES
$300 child-support payments	$500 child care
800 salary (after taxes)	500 apartment
	150 transportation (car)
	160 food
	100 medical expense
$1,100 total	$1,410 total

This budget did not include clothing, entertainment or emergency items. Although Mary struggled to hold her spending to basic survival, using beans, rice, and cheese as food staples and relying on hand-me-down clothes from relatives and friends, she still found herself drawing $400 per month from her savings; she was terrified to consider what would happen when the money ran out.

It was 1982 when I again met with Mary, four years after the divorce. Her situation had changed, but not improved. The children were now both in school and needed only after-school care, reducing child-care expenses to $200, but her car and her money had run out. She now paid an additional $100 a month toward the purchase of a used car. Her salary had increased modestly, but so had rent and food. Jim had been faithful about the $300-a-month child support, but every year when the issue of increased child support came up he managed to show little or no income on his tax returns. She did not have the money to hire a lawyer and challenge him in court.

"I suppose I am not at the poverty level," Mary sighed, "and I know there are many people worse off than I am, but when I can't afford to take the kids out for pizza, and there is no money for gifts when they are invited to a birthday party, it feels poor."

Mary now has no resources except relatives in case of emergency expenses and often ends the month with a family diet of tuna-fish and peanut-butter sandwiches. She feels powerless to improve her position. "A better position came open at the library, but it required a master's degree. They all do. There is no way that I can leave my job to get a master's or retrain. We'd starve. There are no master's programs at night, and if there were I couldn't leave my kids."

Mary Ludden had the misfortune of marrying and becoming a mother in the enlightened seventies, which was supposed to be a decade of new beginnings and triumph for women. If she had married twenty years earlier in the "conservative" fifties, now the object of both scorn and nostalgia, her situation would have been very different. She would have helped Jim through law school, although she would probably not have continued working after the birth of her first child. If Jim had grown restless and desirous of "finding himself" (this would not have been so likely in the corporate spirit of the fifties), he would have considered the option of divorce more thoughtfully. In the first place, his family, his friends, and his church (Mary and Jim are Catholic) would have been censorious. They would have clearly let him know they considered him morally at fault.

If Jim had persisted in the face of social censure and left Mary and the children for a new start in Los Angeles, he would have been treated very differently by the courts under the old laws. If Mary refused to agree to a divorce, the courts could have refused to grant it. Mary would probably have agreed eventually, but on her terms. She would certainly have kept the family home as her own and could have asked for a combination of alimony and child support totaling 60 or 70 percent of Jim's real income. She would not be forced to accept the paper losses shown on his tax return.

And Mary could have expected a great deal of support and sympathy from family and friends, rather than the awkward coolness that follows no-fault divorce. Her life would have been difficult, but it would have been softened by less financial distress and more social support.

When I asked Mary—still an attractive woman at thirty-three—about her social life, she sighed and said, "Sometimes I date, but to be honest I can't afford to pay for the baby-sitter even when my date pays for dinner—and some don't even want to pay for the dinner. Most of the time I'm too tired to think about it. Maybe when the kids get older."

We are now being overwhelmed by hard data, all of it bad news, about the effects of no-fault on women and children. California, the no-fault leader, now offers over ten years of observable evidence. The California Divorce Law Research Project, headed by Lenore Weitzman, has carefully analyzed all divorces since 1970 and has produced some startling statistics. No matter what income level they began in, divorced wives and their children experience extreme downward mobility— averaging a 73 percent lessened standard of living one year following the divorce, while ex-husbands improve their standard of living during this same period by a rise of 42 percent.[17] The man's income may be less than during the marriage, but he has only himself to spend it on. The woman's income will usually be far less than half of their married income, and in 90 percent of the cases she will have the children to care for. Men become single and women become single parents.

In yet another aberration of the concept of equality, spousal support (California's euphemism for alimony) is given to only 17 percent of divorcing spouses, and most often this is too little money for too little time (an average of $217 a month for two years).[18] Spousal support for younger women has almost been extinguished. This was not a requirement of the law, and in fact the law specifically directs the court to consider the effects of employment on dependent children.[19] It is rather a distortion of the egalitarian climate which heralds the self-sufficiency of women. Before no-fault it was considered self-evident that women with children needed protection. With child-care responsibilities, they could not expect to compete equally in the marketplace. Judges, who by and large reflect the attitudes of the prevailing social climate, now believe in the self-sufficiency of women.

Mary and her divorced peers are caught in a three-way bind. First, the law in California and many other states clearly mandates an equal division of property, which often means the wife loses the family home. In pre-no-fault days the mother and the children would have been granted the home at least until the children reached adulthood. Second, the judges have decided that women, whatever their circumstances, can support themselves. And, third, fathers for the most part do not pay even minimal child support. The reasons for fathers' nonpayment certainly precede no-fault divorce, but are buttressed by the moral lassitude it fosters.

Mary might be considered fortunate compared with her peers among newly divorced single mothers. Her husband actually pays the support he was ordered to pay, and she had some savings to draw on. Although the quality of her life is meager, she is a long way from being counted as officially poor. What if her husband stopped paying, or she lost her job and, with her limited skills, could not find another above minimum wage? She would then fall into the so-called "safety net" of social welfare.

AFDC (Aid to Families with Dependent Children) and associated programs are still seen in the suspicious public eye as aid for the chronically poor. Increasingly they are relied upon by formerly middle-class women. The California legislature, alarmed by the fact that women were seeking public assistance in growing numbers, sponsored a series of public hearings with the newly fashioned term "The Feminization of Poverty." The sad stories of middle-age abandonment and single parents' struggles to support children poured forth. Most striking was the anger and amazement of women who had always enjoyed middle-class status and now were forced to endure the indignities of poverty.

Marsha Nolfi (her real name), mother of five, whose professional, high-income husband left her with no support after thirteen years, conveys some of the psychological shock of falling into the welfare world:

"My monthly grant was less than the house payment; needless to say the family home was sold. With such a drastic reduction in income it was necessary for us to

move into a low-income, high-crime area of the city . . .
For me the very process of applying for aid was a sym-
bolic stripping of my integrity and self-esteem. My
financial privacy and the right to interact freely with
the economic system were exchanged for a less-than-
subsistence monthly payment; from now on any money
earned, gifts received or any kind of aid must be reported. . . . The social respect to which I was previously accustomed, in fact, which I never realized was
mine, was now replaced by suspicious and abrupt treatment. It was now difficult to cash a check."[20]

How could this near-Armageddon for women and children occur? The answer is that no-fault occurred more
or less by default. No national soul-searching or debate
took place; the divorce issue did not appear on any
state or national political party's platform, no major
candidate made it a campaign issue. Most Americans
were totally unaware of the widesweeping changes in
family law—and still are. They knew only that it was
now possible to divorce easily and without social con-
tempt.

Family law exists in the backwash of mainstream
American law. Any significant change in antitrust law,
tax law, or criminal procedure is scrutinized by sections
of the bar, by interested lobbying groups, and by constitutional scholars. Most lawyers are not up to date on
the family law of their own state and are not interested
in becoming so. Family law is considered poor paying
and difficult. Few lawyers enjoy hand-holding, and most
are glad to leave the messy business of divorce to sole
practitioners who need the clients.

No-fault divorce galloped through most state legislatures with surprisingly little scrutiny. It was the thing to
do. The input of women into the no-fault stampede has
been too little and too late. In most states nearly all-
male committees of the bar made their recommenda-

tions to nearly all-male legislatures, and they became law. Feminists widely supported the idea of no-fault, since it fit well into their egalitarian framework, and they spent their energy on achieving equality in the marketplace. Only recently have feminist organizations and women's bar groups realized the devastating effects of laws passed under their approving noses.

The most organized reaction has been in New York State where, five years following no-fault, divorced women are indeed finding themselves in trouble. Predictably, organized women, represented by the National Organization for Women, the League of Women Voters and the state chapter of the Women's Bar Association, are seeking an egalitarian solution for this problem. They are pushing for a presumption of *equal* distribution of marital property (the California way), rather than an *equitable* division (taking into consideration all factors).[21]

But an equal division of marital property makes sense only when there is a great deal of property. For most families their home is their major asset. The California experience makes it clear that an equal split most often means selling the house and moving to smaller and poorer quarters. This is a great hardship for the children as well as the mother. Women need to keep their home until their children are grown, and this is more likely accomplished with an equitable (all factors considered) rather than an equal division of property. Beyond that, women with children, and older women whose children are grown, need substantial continuing support from the former husband, when he is capable of providing it.

Supporting an equal rather than an equitable division of property shows a lack of understanding and perhaps concern for the fundamental problems within the no-fault-divorce revolution: the devaluation of the family, the full responsibility of younger women to support their children, the impact of divorce on children of divorce.

The impact of the divorce revolution is a clear example of how an equal-rights orientation has failed women. A women's-rights approach, with an emphasis on protecting the family and recognizing the nearly lifelong commitment of motherhood, would have produced an active united front of women looking out for their own best interests before the catastrophe occurred.

The institution of marriage has been legally transformed without anyone, certainly not feminists, questioning society's stake in marriage. The law has effectively deregulated marriage by asking no questions before granting a divorce and by refusing to impose long-term spousal support. Only with child support has there been a recent renewed concern for enforcement.

In this age of individuality we have lost sight of why the law has any business in regulating marriage. But as the Supreme Court stated in *Skinner v. Oklahoma* in 1937, "Marriage and procreation are fundamental to the very existence and survival of the race . . . Marital intercourse, so that children may be born, is an obligation of the marriage contract, and . . . the foundation upon which must rest the perpetuation of society and civilization."[22]

It is accepted that society as well as the family has a legitimate interest in protecting children. We insist that children be educated to a certain age and we provide free education for this purpose; we remove children from extremely abusive homes, we protect them from employers who would have them working too young or too long, and we provide basic economic support through AFDC and other social-support systems when their parents cannot do so.

Until recently we also protected children by regulating marriage. The strict prohibitions against divorce were to protect the stability of the family, since society was in general agreement that the nuclear family was the best arrangement for raising children. No doubt many partners were miserable in their marriages, but they could not assume that divorce would bring happiness, or that their wishes were paramount. When marriages did end, the law tried to continue family stability for the children as much as possible by insisting that their same lifestyle be maintained. The children were the focus of concern in dividing property and determining continuing support.

Without much thought, or any vote, the law and society seem to be giving up on protecting the nuclear family (mother, father, children) as the main vehicle for raising children. Until recently this was the revered American ideal. The nuclear family may have its warts, but it is a durable institution. Family historian Carl Degler points out that the form of the modern American nuclear family was shaped around the time of the American Revolution. This form includes an affectional bond between spouses, the mother as the primary child-rearer, and smaller families with greater attention to childhood as a time for special attention and education. Earlier versions of the nuclear family, as differentiated from the extended family with generations sharing a household, became the norm in Western Europe from the time of the Reformation in the sixteenth century.[23]

The alternatives to raising children in a nuclear family are not attractive. The major alternative, usually the consequence of divorce, not of choice, is the single-parent household. Such households present the obvious statistical disadvantage of having a greater than 50 percent chance of falling into the dark area below the poverty line. The single-parent family in poverty is expensive for society. Single-parent households above the poverty line may not be a burden on society, but they share a common problem: more work than one adult can manage. Other alternatives suggested by some feminists are communal living arrangements and homosexual marriages. But these are too few in number and experience in America for a considered judgment to be made about them.

Abstractly, society has a strong and legitimate interest in actively promoting the nuclear family as the preferred haven for raising the children who will take charge of the future. Immediately and practically, women have an interest in promoting the nuclear family, since they bear the burden if it fails. Promotion of the family should not merely take the form of discouraging divorce but should provide positive models and incentives as well.

Family education in the schools, beginning with preadolescents, should include positive training on the role of nuclear families and the joys and responsibilities of parenthood. The moral implication of choosing a marriage with children and the long-term commitment to the family unit which this entails must be made explicit. In one innovative experiment in a San Francisco family-living high-school class, each teenager, boys and girls alike, was given a "baby" (stuffed doll) to take care of for a week. The "baby" had to be fed and changed several times a day and once during the night, with these activities logged in a journal. Most importantly, the teenager could not go out at night without finding a responsible adult baby-sitter. What began as a lark for many students soon turned into a burden as well as an unforgettable lesson in parental responsibility.

However, the schools alone should not assume this task of family education. Churches and mature family members must specifically teach these values to children. Since many adolescents are not raised in nuclear families, we can no longer assume they will learn by observation.

As part of a positive rethinking of national family policy, the tax structure for married persons should be revised to allow much greater deductions for children, as well as for education, to reflect the needs of modern families. Society should adopt a caregiver income (described in Chapter Five) which would allow financially pressed mothers with infants not to work outside the home and would help all families with the extra expense of new babies. Publicly subsidized child care (also discussed in Chapter Five) for older children should be a right, not a favor, for families with working mothers. Just as we give special home loans for veterans, we could offer special interest rates for married couples with children buying their first home. Guaranteed health services could be offered for maternity and pediatric care for those families who fall into the crack between job-related health benefits and indigent health care. There are many imaginative ways in which family law, in the widest sense of the word, could promote the interests of the family.

These boosts for families will cost money, but they are a bargain if they can stem the trend toward family collapse and the impoverishment of the mother and the children that so often results. Families that break up are far more likely to seek long-term public assistance than intact families. And healthy, secure, educated children are society's best investment in the future.

The legal procedures relating to marriage and divorce must be looked at from a totally fresh viewpoint as well, rather than as plugging holes in a sinking ship. Part of the incentive for deregulating divorce was a recognition that no longer are all marriages first-time marriages with an expectation of children. There are many first marriages where no children are planned;

there are second and third marriages where an assortment of children exist from previous marriages. There are marriages which occur later in life after the children have grown. With longer lives and fewer children, adults may live most of their married lives without children.

No single legal procedure could fit all these variations on the marriage theme, and it is reasonable to propose that the state has an interest in strictly regulating *only* those marriages where there are children. The state's interest in marriage is in the quality and stability of the environment in which children are raised. Marriages where the partners do not want children or have not yet decided to have children can be handled by private individual contracts. The partners can choose to follow the legal contract required for marriages with children, or they can choose to create their own contract or decide on no contract at all.

Part of a new approach to marriage and divorce procedure should be *informed consent*. Most recruits to marriage join the game without knowing the rules. This is not surprising, since the rules have been changing so rapidly. In my own recent survey of college seniors in a California history class, 70 percent recognized that California was a community-property state, but only 10 percent could define what that meant.

In the best scenario, general family education would begin in junior high school, and specific legal issues would be introduced in high school. Family education should receive at least the same amount of respect as driver education. In addition, a regular four- to six-week course on marital rights and responsibilities presented by legal advisers and counselors should be required before marriage. At that time the couple could choose a contract or construct one of their own and be fully informed of the laws relating to marriages with children and marriages without children. Only then would the couple receive a marriage license. Again, the state's interest in promoting stable families far outweighs the extra burden of a few weeks' counseling. The couple could be required to pay for at least part of the counseling as part of the license fee, just as they must pay for a car license or a real-estate sales license.

Most marriages begin without children, and at least for the period before children arrive they could be governed by contract. Contracts would also be suitable for second or third marriages with no children present. A contract could cover all the mutual rights and obligations of the two parties, including how they shared their money and their household duties. It could optionally include areas of understanding which could not be enforced by a court, such as a statement of five- or ten-year goals or an agreement on leisure-time activities. The value of a contract is that many of the unvoiced values or expectations of each party are revealed and do not come as a shock later in marriage. The danger is that the shock coming before marriage may cancel the marriage, but this is a risk worth taking. All contracts would have provisions for renegotiation, arbitration and termination, which would force them into court only as a last resort. This would greatly reduce the divorce load in the courts and allow the judges to concentrate only on divorces where children are involved.

Until very recently antenuptial or premarital contracts were considered unenforceable, since they allegedly promoted divorce. There has been a widespread renunciation of this position, and most states will now recognize them, although some states limit them only to property rights. There is, in fact, a proposal for a Uniform Premarital Agreement Act sponsored by the National Conference of Commissioners on Uniform State Law, indicating the growing popularity of the idea.[24]

With a contract it is possible for a young childless couple to decide that he will put her through medical school, but in the event of divorce he will get either a flat fee for reimbursement or a continuing percentage of her income for a period of years. This is better than he would do with the laws of most states. It is also possible for a professional working couple without children to keep their incomes totally separate, with the understanding that upon divorce there is nothing to divide and no strings left attached. Second or third marriages where the children are grown and each party comes to the marriage with property could be entirely regulated by contract.

Why bother to marry if your relationship can be governed by private contract? The California Supreme Court in *Marvin v. Marvin* enforced a contract between actor Lee Marvin and Michelle Marvin, who were living together but not married. The message of the Marvin decision, however, is that the contract better be in writing and well thought out. Michelle Marvin had no written contract and she did not get a fraction of what she claimed had been orally promised to her. But for many couples marriage is a public and private statement, grounded in tradition, and at least a casual blessing by the state is important. For others, a religious ceremony is critical. With childless marriages the process of marrying would at least assure that a thoughtful contract had been established.

A contract is *not* sufficient in unions where there are children (whether or not the couple are legally married), because protection of children is a critical state interest. For instance, if a couple with children contracted to keep their property completely separate, it could cause a hardship on the custodial parent upon divorce, or upon wife and children during the course of the marriage. The state's guidelines may be considered the *minimum* when the union is terminated. A couple may choose to contract to give each other and the children *more* than the minimum set by the state; for instance, one partner could promise to pay for the college educations of children over eighteen out of separate property. (Currently there is no child-support obligation after the age of eighteen.)

The position of the state in regulating marriage, divorce, and property settlements (custody will be treated in the next chapter) should always be *the best interest of the children.* During the marriage the issues of who works and who takes care of the children should be left up to the parents, but all income should be considered family income and used to promote the welfare of the family. (This is similar to the concept of community property, but in this case it applies only to communities with children.)

The state is rarely called upon to regulate what goes on in a well-functioning family. It is only with trouble that it intercedes. When trouble occurs, it is in the interest of the state to discourage divorce as the only solution. Required counseling and a long (two-year) separation before divorce should be the minimum requirements for divorce. Even if it were desirable, it is probably no longer possible to require fault as grounds for divorce; but desertion or other grievous acts may be considered in determining a property division, as long as this does not affect the welfare of the children.

The main consideration in determining property division and support must be the children. This is a very different focus from determining who earned what in the marriage, or mandating an equal division. It may mean that the custodial parent, usually the mother, will acquire more than half of the family property, at least until the children are grown (this could be the house and most of the savings). In terms of support, the general guideline should be that the lifestyle of the custodial parent and children should not fall below that of the noncustodial parent. In some cases, this will mean that as the noncustodial parent's career soars, the level of support for the children will also be raised. In other cases (far rarer), the noncustodial parent's obligations would be reduced if the custodial parent enjoyed economic success or the windfall of inheritance. This is, of course, introducing a hornet's nest of complicated calculations, but it is better than the current tragedy of a wife and children falling into poverty while the husband remains affluent.

The true mettle of the law will be tested in dealing with remarriage and stepparent arrangements. As long as there are children in the marriage, the state must be involved. At the outset of the marriage the obligations of the stepparent must be made clear. This may be a sliding scale of responsibility depending upon the natural parent's obligations. The natural parent's obligation may be reduced if the economic condition of his or her children and former spouse are greatly enhanced by remarriage. In case of divorce where a stepparent is involved, the same standard of the interest of the children must be imposed. This could be more than a potential stepparent is willing to take on, but that issue should be faced at the beginning of a marriage.

The older displaced homemaker, the object of much media attention but little practical relief, should be given full consideration even though the children are no longer her daily responsibility. In the interest of promoting the family, the caretaking parent must be certain that the years in which she gives first priority to child-caring will not result in an impoverished old age. The wife of a twenty-year or more marriage in which there were children must be assured that a decent standard of living, in keeping with her previous economic status, will be permanently assured following divorce. This may, of course, entail a sharp reduction when the husband retires; but her share in his pension should be guaranteed. (This would also apply to the husband in the small number of cases where he was the caretaker.) Even women who work full time during the child-raising years rarely have the time to pursue the more lucrative jobs which require more hours and more responsibility. This support may be accomplished either through property division (if there is enough property) or by continuing alimony. If the woman has not worked during marriage she should be encouraged to do so when possible. (These options will be discussed in the chapter on reentry women.) In most circumstances reentry women command low wages which must be supplemented by the former spouse.

Family law should be offered as the first plank in a women's-rights platform, replacing the total disregard it has received on the equal-rights agenda. Divorce is an issue around which all women, egalitarians and conservatives alike, can rally. Husbands and fathers, who also suffer the loss of family as a result of divorce, will also respond. The consequences of divorce on the lives of children can be the issue that cuts across ideological and gender lines.

Carrying out family-law reform is made difficult by the fact that marriage and divorce are traditionally regulated by the states, with almost no federal interference. Only recently, with the federal law enforcing child support, has the federal government stepped into the family-law scene. Family law is considered one of the last sacred refuges of states' rights. We have fifty states, one district, and two territories, each with their own version of family law. With marriage, divorce, and custody law, the discrepancies among them are shocking. Since women and men rarely choose the state of their residence for its divorce laws, the results are quite unfair. Here is an example where the elastic concept of equality—as in equality of treatment between states (not equality with men)—would be useful.

Although it is desirable to have a uniform national policy regarding marriage and divorce, the difficulty in taking this power away from the states and giving it to the federal government is formidable. Creating a constitutional rationale for federal supremacy in matters of divorce and custody runs up against the stony wall of history and precedent. The end run which allows state laws to become uniform, or nearly uniform, is the adoption, state by state, of uniform laws. This has been done most successfully (after many years it has been adopted by all states) with the Uniform Child Custody Jurisdiction Act, which mandates that a state must enforce a custody order from another state.

Well-organized women and men of all political persuasions are in a good position to draft a Uniform Family Law (working with the National Conference of Commissioners on Uniform State Law) and to hurry it through the legislature of each state. The same spirit that rallied forces in state legislatures for the ERA could effectively reform family law.

On the federal level, organized men and women could tackle Congress and insist upon family-law reforms in the areas of tax advantages, low-cost interest rates, family-support systems, and family education in the schools, as well as a systematic review of all laws, regulations, and rules for their impacts on families.

As a nation we do not have to sit passively and watch families fall apart. It is possible to actively pursue a national policy which views the nuclear family as the best environment for raising children and promotes that ideal in every way possible.

3

SOLOMON'S SOLUTION: JOINT CUSTODY

> *. . . And when they had brought a sword before the king, he said, "Divide the living child in two and give half to the one, and half to the other." But the woman whose child was alive said to the king, "I beseech thee, my lord, give her the child alive and do not kill it." But the other said, "Let it be neither mine nor thine, but divide it."*
>
> —1 Kings 3:24–26

Ten years after it pioneered the no-fault revolution in 1970, California logically extended the egalitarian idea to joint custody of children, thereby dividing the living child in two, and the rest of the nation, once again, is racing to follow the leader. Over thirty states have passed statutes bearing on joint custody, and several others have proposals before their legislatures.[1] Dr. John Haynes, president of the Academy of Family Mediators, predicts, "Within five years joint parenting will be the norm, even within the court system."[2]

If the current rate of divorce continues, about half of the children under eighteen will experience divorce by 1990.[3] Without any public debate or national research on the subject, state legislatures are making decisions regarding custody which could affect half the children of this nation.

Feminist groups have shown little interest in custody issues. They have given up their historical role as advocates for children and focused instead on women's success in the marketplace. The move toward joint custody has been led almost entirely by fathers'-rights organizations.

California's custody law, enacted in 1980, gives first preference to joint custody. Where the parents agree to joint custody, there "shall be a presumption . . . that joint custody is in the best interest of the child." Furthermore, the court may, in its discretion, award joint custody when only *one parent* requests it! The law also states the unsupported presumption that if only one parent seeks joint custody, such a parent is more apt to see that the child has frequent and continuing contact with the other parent—the so-called "friendly parent" assumption.[4] Although the law is relatively new and courts move at a glacial pace, there is already one appellate-court decision which supports a joint-custody award imposed over the objection of the mother (*In re Marriage of Wood*).[5] So far, seven states have followed the California lead: the judge can impose joint custody over the objection of one parent.

There are many things wrong with this unthinking rush to joint custody, but the primary objection is that it changes the focus of custody away from the "best interests of the child" to the best interests of the parents—or, more precisely, to the best interests of the father. With no-fault divorce each partner is equally responsible (or equally not responsible) and equally capable of taking care of him- or herself; now each parent is equally "fit" and equally entitled to custody.

As Justice Felice K. Shea pointed out in a 1978 New York joint-custody decision, *Dodd v. Dodd:*

> Joint custody is an appealing concept. It permits the court to escape an agonizing choice, to keep from wounding the self-esteem of either parent and to avoid the appearance of discrimination between the sexes. Joint custody allows parents to have an equal voice in making decisions and it recognizes the advantage of shared responsibility for raising the young. But serious questions remain to be answered. How does joint custody affect the children? What are the factors to be considered and weighed?[6]

In the American tradition of flexibility, our courts have held three completely different beliefs about what is in the best interest of children over the past three decades. In the fifties it was common wisdom that children were almost always best off in an intact family and the parents must sacrifice their own happiness and avoid divorce. In the sixties and seventies it became accepted dogma that children were happy only if their parents were happy and that divorce was always preferable to an unhappy marriage; but the mother was almost always given custody. In the eighties it is becoming dogma that children are happiest when they spend equal time in the household of each parent following divorce.

The hard truth is that we have very few studies of children in traditional custodial arrangements, and almost *no* evidence on the effects of joint custody on children.[7] Yet, as a nation we are willing to follow the fad of joint custody and use our children as guinea pigs in a new experiment.

A study often quoted in favor of joint custody is *Surviving the Breakup*, by Judith S. Wallerstein and Joan Berlin Kelly, a thorough five-year follow-through of sixty families and 131 children of divorce. It is currently the most complete study available on the effects of divorce on children. One of the conclusions of this study is "the desirability of the child's continuing relationship with both parents during the postdivorce years in an arrangement which enables each parent to be responsible for and genuinely concerned with the well-being of the children."[8] The authors go on to recommend joint *legal* custody, which in California is a separate concept from joint *physical* custody. This very loosely defined concept gives both parents access to school records and gives them joint rights when legal permission is necessary, such as medical operations. It is a very different concept from joint physical custody, which gives parents equal rights to the child himself.

Wallerstein is strongly opposed to the use of their study by the advocates of joint physical custody, and insists the study never recommended that joint physical custody should be imposed on the parents without their total agreement. She is concerned that social policy is being dictated without adequate research. Some children, she claims, are likely to become the victims of a "no-child's land" between two hostile parents.[9]

How does joint custody work? It can take many forms: alternate weeks, alternate days, alternate years, or the parents can travel back and forth from their separate residences while the kids stay in the house or apartment. Sometimes these children are still in diapers and not yet walking. This is the evolution of the truly egalitarian family where the parents are equal and autonomous, each with a full-time job and part-time children. It is the children who must accommodate to their parents' separate lives and lifestyles.

My own experience with custody following divorce, shared by most of my clients and friends, is that the best that one can hope for is a quiet truce and a very reliable visitation schedule. It is fruitless and usually provocative to try to agree upon junk food, pajama-wearing, and all the other trivial details that make up a child's familiar environment. All of the affection and generosity that allow parents to make decisions in an intact family are absent. Communication is cut to the bare minimum to avoid an outbreak of hostility. It is hard to understand how joint custody could completely turn around the strained relations between adults who divorced presumably because they could not get along with each other, and allow the interchange and agreement on details which would establish real continuity between the child's two lives.

Not only has joint custody not been proven to be in the best interests of children; it has been used as a weapon against women to reduce or eliminate child-support payments. The logic is elementary: "We can both work to support ourselves, and now that we share the children equally we will each pay for them when they are with us." The flaw in this logic is that women almost universally earn far less money and must maintain a household large enough for children whether or not children are present.

Another version on this theme is the threat "If you ask for dollars in child support or spousal support, I will ask for joint custody." A California attorney who mainly represents men in divorce suits admitted to me, "About sixty percent of my male clients ask for joint custody now, but only about ten percent really want it. It's a good bargaining position."

Since the law in California states that custody orders made before 1980 can be reviewed again in favor of joint custody, there has been a good deal of renegotiating and some severe arm-twisting among long-divorced couples. Gerry, a young woman friend, came to me for advice. Gerry became pregnant and was married at fourteen (with her parents' consent), to a nineteen-year-old youth. They lived with her parents for a time after the first child was born and then moved to the Southwest, where a second child was born. Her husband was at best an unstable provider. At worst he was violent and sporadically involved in drug-dealing, often bringing home his criminal associates. Gerry finally left him on her twentieth birthday, in 1978. "I was afraid he would kill me and the kids, I couldn't sleep for weeks," she recalled.

She returned to her hometown, and he eventually followed, demanding to see the children. Since he now seemed to be making money, ostensibly in an auto repair shop, she insisted upon child support. He paid for a few months and then stopped. After two years she took him to court and received a judgment for back support of several thousand dollars. He retaliated, threatening that he would seek joint custody under the new law if she did not drop the issue of back support.

Gerry is terrified. She is certain he is still involved with criminal activities and fears that he may turn his violence against the children. She sought her attorney's advice and was given the harsh news that the judge could well grant joint custody, since her husband appeared financially capable and had remarried, giving the appearance, at least, of domestic stability. Gerry quickly dropped her claim for back support and is considering moving out of town to escape his demand for joint custody.

A continuance of the parent–child relationship for

both parents is surely desirable, but joint physical custody is not the general solution. At best it can work for a tiny minority of parents thoroughly committed to it; it can never be the judicially preferred solution, nor should it be imposed by the court upon unwilling partners.

The strict criteria set down by an Iowa court provide a good guideline for the family situation in which joint custody is appropriate:

1. Each parent must be fit and suitable to take custody.

2. The parties must agree to take joint custody and be capable of reaching shared decisions in the children's best interest.

3. There must be geographic proximity so as not to substantially disrupt children's schooling and other routines.

4. The environment of each of the parental homes must be similar.

5. There must be no indication that the psychological or emotional needs of the children would suffer under a joint custody arrangement.

6. The work hours of each parent must permit such a custodial arrangement.

7. Joint custody must not be strongly opposed by the children.[10]

There is, however, a strong contingent among mental-health professionals that firmly believe that joint custody is *never* in the best interests of the child. Joseph Goldstein, Anna Freud, and Albert Solnit, in their highly influential work *Beyond the Best Interests of the Child,* argue the essential role of the "psychological parent" in the healthy development of every child. The psychological parent may not be the biological parent, but it is the adult with whom the child is personally and emotionally involved. The authors hold that emotional continuity is critical to the child's development and that only one parent must be given custody. This parent has the right to control or exclude visits by the non-custodial parent as they wish.

> Children have difficulty in relating positively to, profiting from, and maintaining the contact with two psychological parents who are not in positive contact with each other. Loyalty conflicts are common and normal under such conditions and may have devastating consequences by destroying the child's positive relationships to both parents. A "visiting" or "visited" parent has little chance to serve as a true object for love, trust, and identification, since this role is based on his being available on an uninterrupted day-to-day basis. Once it is determined who will be the custodial parent, it is that parent, not the court, who must decide under what conditions he or she wishes to raise the child. Thus, the noncustodial parent should have no legally enforceable right to visit the child, and the custodial parent should have the right to decide whether it is desirable to have such visits.[11]

Clearly there is no happy solution to the agonizing problem of which parent gets the child when joint custody is not appropriate, as it rarely is. Solomon, in his wisdom, believed that a real parent would be more concerned about the welfare of her child than about her own welfare. In the turmoil and bitterness of divorce this is not always the case.

Historically, the law relating to custody has been a clear reflection of prevailing social attitudes toward the role of men and women in child-rearing. Under English common law the father was considered the natural guardian of the children and controlled their education and training. Child care was seen primarily in terms of child-training. If the couple separated, the father was given custody; it was considered his "natural right." As fathers moved off the farm and went to work in the city, mothers became full-time caretakers, and judges began to see the mother as "naturally" responsible for the children.[12]

By the twentieth century judicial decisions in America had firmly established the preference for mothers as custodians of their children after divorce, particularly if the children were of "tender years." Child care now was seen primarily as nurturance and love, since the function of education and training had been assumed by the schools. For more than fifty years this preference was rarely questioned and was given the respect of natural law. As one Idaho court said of the maternal preference, it "needs no argument to support it because it arises out of the very nature and instincts of motherhood; Nature has ordained it."[13]

The egalitarian momentum which pushed through no-fault divorce directly challenged maternal preference. In California, for instance, the statutory language was changed from an explicit maternal preference to "the best interest of the child" in 1973. Almost all state legislatures, facing the same egalitarian pressures, rushed to change the language of their statutes from maternal preference to "the best interest of the child," but they provided no guidelines to the courts as to what that meant. This forced well-meaning but ill-prepared judges to determine what they considered the best interests of the child on a case-by-case basis.

The fact that fathers in the seventies were awarded sole physical custody only 10 percent of the time largely reflects the fact that fathers generally do not seek sole custody. The reasons for this are complex, including the reluctance to endure the nasty business of a custody battle, but the truth is that most men, no matter how attached they are to their children, are not willing to take on the everyday responsibility of raising them.[14]

The man who does take on the responsibility of the children is perceived as an heroic figure. The single-parent phenomenon rated the journalistic attention of a *Newsweek* cover in 1985. Of the four single-parent families portrayed, the most prominently covered was a father with two small children. This father, Dan Jones, had not sued for custody; his wife had made the decision that two young children were too much responsibility for her. A good deal of the article focuses on his ability to find matching socks in the laundry and on his cooking ability; "I am great at mixing slop," he boasts. In contrast, the portraits of the single parent families headed by women concentrate on their financial hardships and problems with relationships.[15]

We all know families in which the father is indeed the more nurturing parent and often the prime caretaker; we may even know families in which that father sought custody. Men who do seek sole custody have an increasingly good chance of obtaining it. In an effort to be modern and nonsexist, judges are sometimes too willing to lean toward fathers. A California study in 1977 demonstrated that 63 percent of divorced fathers who requested sole physical custody of their children were awarded it (often by the mother's agreement without a full contest).[16] This represents an increase from 35 percent in 1968.

And yet few men voluntarily choose the hard road of single parenting if the mother is fit. In a survey of recently divorced California men with children under eighteen, 40 percent indicated that they have never thought of having custody of their children and if given the option would simply reject it. Another 20 percent reported having positive thoughts about having their children with them after divorce, but when they are "being practical" they are not willing to assume sole custody. The remaining 40 percent stated that at some point in their divorce proceeding they seriously considered seeking custody but were dissuaded by their wives, their lawyers, and their own realization of the practical and financial difficulties they would encounter. Finally, only about one father in eight decided to seek sole custody.[17]

When the easy choice of joint physical custody is not an option, and mother and father both fight to gain physical custody, judges are at a loss. What is in "the best interest of the child"? Are mothers naturally more nurturing, more caretaking, than fathers? Can fathers provide better models for sons and mothers for daughters? Should the material quality of life the child would enjoy with the wealthier parent be a consideration? Are the moral and religious values of the parent an important factor?

David Chambers, law professor and respected theorist in the area of custody, has recommended that legislatures give a clear-cut preference to the primary caretaker up to the child's age of six. The primary caretaker is the parent who performs the majority of the everyday tasks of feeding, clothing, and general maintenance. The primary caretaker is the parent who notices when the toes of the child are pushing through the end of his sneakers.

Chambers, following a close examination of current scientific studies, finds that there is no clear-cut biological or psychological evidence which points to the mother rather than the father as a more fit caretaker; but in this culture, as in most, caretaking is usually the mother's role. Chambers also points to the growing body of studies which focus on the importance to the child of the secondary caretaker, most often the father.

. . . there is a large and widely accepted body of writing by developmental psychologists that concludes that there is typically a special attachment between a young child and a primary caretaker and foresees subtle, but significant harm from its breach. Research on the ties of children to secondary caretakers makes clear that such ties are stronger than previously believed but leaves open the significant possibility that preserving the intimate interaction of the primary caretaker is of greater importance to the child.[18]

The child's best interest comes first, but a secondary justification which Chambers offers for a primary-caretaker presumption is fairness to the primary caretaker, who may lose not just the child but a great part of the structure and purpose of daily life. Chambers quotes a woman speaking about her own divorce: "He is an excellent parent, but they are the most important thing in my life, and I would not have survived without them. They would have been happy either way, but I wouldn't have pulled through if I had lost them."[19]

Between the ages of six and twelve Chambers offers no statutory guidelines, taking the position that the evidence of attachment of children to the primary caretaker becomes weaker with age. (But this does not take into account the attachment of the primary caretaker to the child, which may not weaken with age.) After the age of twelve, he feels, children can make at least as good judgments about which parent is in their own best interest as the court can.

Chambers strongly recommends that legislatures *forbid* the imposition of joint physical custody over the objection of one parent. The complete absence of studies of the effects of imposed joint custody upon children plus the obvious difficulties of such arrangements rule it out completely. He is mildly approving of voluntary joint physical custody under strictly limited circumstances and only for children over the age of three.[20]

Chambers' guidelines represent the first effort to replace the arbitrary judgments of the court with firm guidelines based on scientific evidence. He is continually stymied, as are all policymakers in this field, by the lack of thorough research on what must be considered one of America's most pressing problems.

The problem of deciding who gets the child after divorce is accentuated by the gravely inadequate decision-making mechanism. When custody is disputed, or custody-related matters such as visitation are disputed, the imposition of joint custody is certainly not the answer and a traditional judge may not be the one to find the solution. The results of an in-depth study of judicial attitudes toward custody in Kentucky revealed that most judges felt inadequate to deal with the deluge of custody disputes that are now laid at their bench. One judge expressed the feelings of many: "This area of law is the most difficult and time-consuming and getting worse." Many judges were frustrated because each case had to be decided on its own merits, rather than based on well-worn precedents. When everything was taken into consideration they admitted it was gut reaction that decided the ruling. They felt that they had no special training for making such judgments, and that at times they felt angry for being forced to make such important decisions concerning a child.[21]

An adversarial system may be quite effective in determining who breached a construction contract, but it has serious limitations in determining who should get custody of the children. The interests of each parent are usually represented by a paid attorney, and perhaps paid expert witnesses, but no one is hired to represent the interests of the children. A variety of different approaches are possible, and nearly all of them are preferable to the traditional adversarial model. One approach is to appoint an advocate for the child—an attorney who, with the help of mental-health professionals, can bridge the gap between the law and the psychological needs of the child. Specially trained mental-health professionals are currently a luxury found only in the most sophisticated courts of the largest cities.

The most popular trend is mediation, again led by California, where it is now *mandatory* in all issues regarding custody and visitation, but not support.[22] The mediators are mental-health professionals—not lawyers—chosen by the courts. They work with the parents to develop a pattern of custody and visitation outside the courtroom. The agreement is then presented to the judge, who almost never overrides it. An agreement is reached in the great majority of cases.

But the mediator often becomes an authority figure even more powerful than the judge, and, without the support of the individual attorneys (who are most often banned from the mediation session), the mediator's bias can overwhelm the confused couple. The legal preference in California is for joint physical custody, and this is often what the mediator will recommend. In some counties where there is strong pressure from both judge and mediator, a majority of couples decide on joint physical custody.[23] Given the strict criteria for workable joint custody described above, it is highly unlikely that so high a percentage of couples are in fact suited to joint custody.

Once joint custody is agreed upon, it is almost impossible to get the court to reverse the agreement. Divorce expert Wallerstein, who was involved in setting up the mediation process in California, related the story of a clearly psychotic mother who sometimes bit her three-year-old child, yet when called to court she made a good appearance and the judge refused to rescind the joint-custody order.[24]

Sadly, sexual abuse is frequently charged by one parent in order to wrest sole physical custody from the other. Fathers, and sometimes mothers, are increasingly subject to false accusations that they sexually molested their children. Because such accusations are so frequent and so often false, judges virtually always dismiss them. This tends to discredit real cases of sexual abuse which occur outside of custody situations.[25]

At the 1986 annual meeting of the American Academy of Child and Adolescent Psychiatry, the alarming increase in the number of sexual-molestation cases was attributed to a greater public awareness of sexual abuse, laws requiring teachers and doctors to report even unsubstantiated accusations, careless counselors who interview purported victims with leading questions, and joint-custody laws that in some cases lead mothers to fight harder for sole custody of their children.[26]

Clearly the future of our children depends on some hard rethinking and solid research regarding the effect of divorce and custody on children. We can afford basic studies on the 50 percent of children who will experience divorce; in fact, we cannot afford to do without them.

Without hard evidence that splitting the residence of the children equally between the parents is good for the children, joint custody should *not* be given legislative preference—the current trend in the law. It should *never* be imposed without the full consent of both parents and without the presence of other critical factors which assure a smooth continuity between the households. The old California solutions of joint *legal* custody with sole *physical* custody worked fairly well in establishing the rights of the noncustodial parent without treating the child as a football.

When custody is contested, a nonadversarial situation must be devised in which all parties, including the child, receive counseling and representation. A judge who specializes solely in family law and has an appropriate counseling background could hear all custody disputes. The judge should have some specific guidelines from the legislature as to what factors must be considered to be in the best interest of the child. These should include a preference for the primary caretaker, at least for young children.

Each party, including the child, must be free to return to court to review the arrangement if it is not working for her or him. There will be no perfect solution for every party in this impossible dilemma, but there must be a recognition that the child, not the mother or the father, is the most important party.

It is already clear that the effects of divorce on children do not end with the custody decision. The Wallerstein and Kelly study indicates that after five years 37 percent of the children of divorce were moderately to severely depressed. An important aspect of their mental health was the degree of support they received during the separation and following the divorce. A full four-fifths of the youngest children were not provided with either an adequate explanation of the divorce or assurance of continued care. The parents were usually so preoccupied with their own overwhelming problems that they could not deal with the needs of their children. Fewer than 10 percent received adult help from their community or from family friends, and fewer than 5 percent were counseled by a church congregation or a minister.[27]

One of the most severe, continuing strains on children and their custodial parent, usually the mother, is the constant economic worry and, for many, the sure slide into poverty. The fact that 54 percent of single-parent families now live below the poverty line does not tell the story of the economic struggles of the other 46 percent who are holding their heads up somewhere above this line.

Most children are forced to abandon the family home. About 60 percent relocate to more affordable housing within two years. For many this means leaving a comfortable home and a familiar neighborhood for a small rented apartment. Small children often take on the economic worries of their single parent. As family counselor Catherine Blusiewicz observed, "I get nine- and ten-year-olds coming in who talk about the light bill, the rent's due . . . They've got the same worried look their parents have. They're like little miniature adults."[28]

Their single parent is often harassed beyond endurance, attempting to act as breadwinner and homemaker with too little money for the luxury of household help or a dinner at a restaurant. This reduces both the quantity and the quality of parenting that is available to the children. It is not surprising that for many years following the divorce most children yearn for reconciliation and a return to an intact family.[29]

A major factor in the deteriorated quality of life for children after divorce is that fewer than half of all fathers who are subject to child-support orders fully comply, and, according to Fred Schutzmann, deputy director of the federal Office of Child Support Enforcement, "Studies show that noncompliance is equal whether you are making $10,000 or $50,000 a year."[30] Nonpaying fathers are perhaps the major reason for the enormous growth in public assistance to women and children. In 1981 the federal child-support system, Aid to Families with Dependent Children, paid benefits to eleven million custodial parents and children, most of whom were potentially eligible for child support. In 1935 when AFDC was created by the Social Security Act, most of the children who benefited were orphans; now the overwhelming majority of the children's mothers are divorced or separated or have not been married.[31]

Whether or not the single parent and the children become "officially poor" is greatly determined by whether or not fathers pay support. A U.S. Census Bureau study in 1979 indicated that one-third of the divorced and separated women who did not receive child support fell below the poverty line compared with 12 percent who received support.[32]

Because nonpaying fathers cost taxpayers money, Congress has pierced the sanctity of states' rights that traditionally surrounds family law and passed firm legislation to force compliance with child-support obligations. In 1975 Congress established the Child Support Enforcement program, with responsibility for running it given to the states. This program authorized the Internal Revenue Service to withhold tax refunds in cases where states certified that the father (or the mother in 5 percent of the cases) was past due on child-support payments. It also subsidized the cost of establishing paternity, locating absent fathers, and collecting child support. In 1980 the use of the IRS for collections was extended to non-AFDC families.[33]

These measures were so successful, netting $1.6 billion, that Congress got tougher in 1984 and passed a law (P.L. 98-378) which set child-support standards that all states must meet if they wish to continue to receive AFDC funds. These standards, in part, require that all states implement a system of automatic wage-withholding for delinquent parents and adopt strict interstate enforcement of support orders.[34]

It seems clear that the main reason child support is not paid is because fathers (and a few mothers) are not forced to pay. Before congressional intervention, mothers had to hire a lawyer and take the father to court in order to get an enforcement order that was often not enforced. Although there are criminal penalties for nonpayment in all states, these are rarely invoked, mainly because jail is obviously counterproductive in this matter—you can't earn wages in prison. The success of wage assignments with delinquent parents leads some reformers to suggest that the court should not wait until the parent is delinquent, but should insist on wage assignments as a part of payroll deduction at the time of the original support order. California already has this statutory option,[35] but it is rarely used.

Even when fathers do pay the amount they are assigned, it is not enough to keep their children from sliding into the gray zone just above "official" poverty. There is an alarming trend toward smaller and smaller child-support awards—a drop of 28.4 percent since 1978.[36] This probably reflects the mistaken judicial presumption that women can support themselves as well as men can. It may also be an early indication of the depressing effect of joint custody on child-support awards. The result is the increasing impoverishment of mothers and children of divorce. The previously noted Weitzman study in California found that divorced women and their children experience a 73 percent reduction in their standard of living while the noncustodial father experiences a 42 percent rise in income relative to his needs.[37]

Since the resources in the family pot often remain the same, these odd statistics are explained by the fact that the relative needs of the individuals sharing the pot change. If the income of the intact Brown family of four totals $40,000 ($30,000 husband's earnings, $10,000 wife's), the postdivorce split will probably be $25,000 husband, $15,000 wife, with $5,000 of the husband's salary going to the wife for child support. Mr. Brown has less money than before, but he has only one mouth to feed and one body to shelter and clothe with that money. His studio apartment and small grocery bill will allow him more disposable income for his own entertainment than he had as a family man. Mrs. Brown now has $15,000 to feed, shelter and clothe three people, where before she had $40,000 to take care of four. Although she is a hair above official poverty, it is not hard to predict her economic woes and the greatly reduced life which will be the children's lot. The fact that one child out of four may fall into official poverty by 1990 is no surprise.

The well-being of the child must always be the primary concern in determining child support, as it must be with custody and divorce law. The problems of child support have been severely affected by the egalitarian divorce reform. Not only are there many more children of divorce following the no-fault revolution, but the virtual elimination of court-awarded spousal support to women with small children has not been balanced by an increase in child support; in fact they have been cut down as well. Child-support payments almost universally cover less than half of the expenses of the child, and the other half is supposed to be picked up by the mother, who rarely has the same earning capacity as the father. The judicial notion that mothers and fathers are equally responsible for supporting the children is based on the egalitarian fallacy that men and women are equally capable of earning money.

A support policy which put the child first would, as much as possible, attempt to prevent disruption of the child's life and lifestyle. This would mean leaving the family home with the custodial parent (even if this did not accomplish an immediate equal distribution of property) and setting support payments so that the child's lifestyle would not fall below that of the non-custodial parent. It would also extend the obligation of both parents past eighteen to include schooling at least until age twenty-one. (The courts regularly end support obligations at eighteen, but it is not a constitutional requirement.) The child's chance at a college education should not be cut off with divorce.

With our hypothetical Brown family, described above, this would probably mean that Mr. Brown would keep an income of $15,000 and Mrs. Brown and the children would have an income of $25,000 ($15,000 in child support). By today's standards, this would seem a very harsh burden for the father. But which scenario is fairer for the children? Parenting is, after all, a lifelong obligation. This burden could be made lighter by a federal tax policy which did not tax child-support payments for either party, or which taxed them at a greatly reduced rate. (Currently the one who pays out support is taxed at full rate.) This would amount to a government subsidy, but would be less expensive than current forms of public assistance.

An important public-policy decision is whether the custodial mother should be forced to work, thereby reducing the support load on the father. Our hypothetical but realistic Mrs. Brown is already working, and typically she does not have the skills or the time to earn much more. If the mother is not working at the time of the divorce, a realistic assessment of her skills, the age of the children, etc., should be made, and an appropriate time for retraining (supported by the husband) should be granted. A woman who is forced into the job market out of immediate necessity will not earn as much as she would following retraining. Given the current sad state of our child-care support system, it is not always economically advantageous for a mother with small children and limited skills to return to work; and it may not be in the best interest of the children. Many small children have chronic health or emotional problems which require full-time parenting.

What about the intact family of four with a net family income of $18,000? No matter how you split that pot, someone or everyone will fall below the poverty line. A guaranteed child allowance must allow for the government (state and federal combined) to make up the deficit so that no child is without a decent standard of living. Aid to Families with Dependent Children is currently the program assigned to provide this; over 45 percent of all children on AFDC (about three million children) are eligible because their parents are divorced or separated.[38]

But no one is pleased with the policy or the performance of AFDC, least of all the people who depend upon it. Recently the Children's Defense Fund stated: "In most states AFDC maximum benefits are intolerably low, failing to provide even a minimum level of decency." Only one state, Alaska, pays minimum benefits that are higher than the poverty threshold.[39] The complex issues involved with reforming AFDC go beyond the problem of child support (and beyond the scope of this book), but clearly the lives of many children following divorce are tied to this inadequate program. It must be changed to provide a decent life for these children.

For those families where there is something to split, who should split the pot? Currently, judges are all-powerful. Most states have a statute that affirms the noncustodial parent's duty to pay support, but the judge determines the actual amount. A few states set forth minimum guidelines, but leave the rest to judicial discretion. Judgments can vary wildly within the same state. Therefore fathers (and mothers) can always find someone with a similar income who pays less, fueling their urge to stop paying entirely. The judgment only rarely includes an inflation clause, putting the burden in most states on the custodial parent to hire a lawyer to seek a redetermination—often paying the lawyer more than the increase.

Strictly developed federal guidelines which allow little judicial discretion in the determination of support awards and which require a frequent review of circumstances (perhaps every two years) are necessary. Ordinary judges, who often handle everything from drunk driving to will contests, are not appropriate decisionmakers for support issues or for custody issues. Many states are moving toward a family-law commissioner or a family-law court where family law matters could be handled routinely and with expertise.

Legislators are often reluctant to pass strict laws regarding support, because they fear it will hit their own pocketbooks. In the California debate over an automatic wage assignment in support decrees, a woman senator commented, "What you have is a committee of men who are very protective of their own . . . I go around and make my tally of who's been divorced, and those who are vehemently opposed are usually those who are faced with child support payments. We're touching a raw nerve."[40] The bill failed in its original tough form.

It is shocking that organized women of all political persuasions have paid so little attention to the deteriorating condition of the nation's children through divorce. An exotic custody case, Baby M and surrogate mother Mary Beth Whitehead, attracted the attention of dozens of prominent feminists, while the everyday fate of hundreds of thousands of children enduring custody disputes has gone virtually unnoticed. It is particularly surprising since it is women that share the poverty and hardship with the children following divorce. Women must resume their historical role as the advocates for children.

A women's-rights as opposed to an equal-rights campaign would emphasize the intertwined fate of women and children. The campaign would push for national research on the effects of divorce and custody on children, and it would seek to block laws that split children's lives in half for no other reason than that it is the egalitarian solution. Continued counseling and community support groups for children of divorce would be high priority, as would government-subsidized childcare and after-school programs for working mothers. A decent standard of living for all children, including the victims of divorce, would be high on the agenda.

4

WHY WOMEN WORK

Recently I attended my twentieth college reunion. As I expected, there was nostalgia. The forgotten yet familiar shine and odor of wax in the formal reception hall pulled me back twenty years. The study stalls in the library recalled the hundreds of hours I spent studying and dreaming.

What I didn't expect was that upon meeting old friends and acquaintances at the welcoming reception I was asked only two questions: "Where do you live?" and "What do you do?" Vassar was still a women's college in 1965, all the reunioners were women, yet no one asked me what my husband did, or indeed whether I had a husband; and no one inquired whether I had children. These would have been the acceptable

opening lines for women attending their twentieth reunion in 1965, the year of my graduation.

More than conversational protocol had changed: a
review of the reunion bulletin revealed that there
were almost no housewives left, at least among those
who responded to the questionnaire. There were a
depressingly large number of lawyers, a large group
whose title was in the nebulous neighborhood of con-
sultant or manager, a small group of university professors and administrators, a smaller group of elementary-
school teachers and social workers, and a tiny group of
physicians.

We were the first group to come of age at the beginning of the egalitarian crusade. I, for one, was al-
ternately reading *Bride* magazine and *The Feminine
Mystique* during May of my senior year. Ours was
the last class to find status in marrying immediately
after college, and the first class to return to law school
when we decided that marriage was not enough. As
individuals we decided somewhere during that twenty
years not just to work, but to work at the kinds of jobs
that our husbands worked at. No longer would we depend upon our husband's status; indeed, no longer
would we depend upon a husband. Our work became
our identity.

Or so it seemed on the first afternoon of reunion
weekend. Back in the dorm, as we refilled our plas-
tic wineglasses late into the night, a different story
emerged.

Demographically, my rooming group of six had ful-
filled all of the statistical expectations of women of
our age and background. We had among the six of
us a total of eight marriages and three divorces (two
remarriages). Four of us had the requisite two children, one had seven stepchildren, and one had no
children at all. Four of us worked full time—two as

lawyers, one as an academic, one as a social-service administrator—and two remained in the home.

Behind the statistics, our talk revealed the confusion we felt about our lives. Not one of us felt she had achieved much in her career; having chosen male careers and judging ourselves by male standards, we had the vague feeling that we were failures. Those who remained in the home felt even less positive about themselves.

There was a great deal of painful talk about children—not just the ordinary problems of child care and garden-variety adolescent rebellion, but serious physical and mental problems that absorbed the mother's total energy. There was also happy talk about children and a consensus that they were the fulcrum that balanced our often uneasy lives. Men occupied our conversation much as they had twenty years ago; but somehow we seemed to have understood them better twenty years ago. Then we had judged men by the status and economic support we predicted they would bring us: "Where does your boyfriend go to school?" "What is he studying?" Now we asked for something different: "How loving will you be?" "Will you help with the children?" There had been too many failed marriages and too many relationships gone sour.

Why have our attitudes about men, work, and our identity changed so drastically since 1965? Why has our entry into the male race for career success brought us ambivalence and confusion as well as some heady moments of satisfaction? Are we the victims or the victors of the egalitarian crusade?

Statistics show that my classmates and I have been swept up by the huge wave of women entering the labor market in the sixties and seventies. Twenty-nine percent of all women were in the work force in 1940, 54 percent in 1984. There was, of course, a brief bulge

caused by women working in factories during the war—
up to 38 percent in 1945, down to 30.8 percent in
1947—but the biggest continuous rise occurred after
1960, when the curve soared from 34 percent to 54
percent in 1984.[1]

Most of these new recruits to the labor force are
married women. Their mothers gave up work upon
acquiring a wedding ring, or certainly with the beginning bulge of the first baby. Now 49 percent of this
generation of mothers resume work before the baby
has begun to teethe.

My five classmates and I, with our eight marriages
and fifteen children (seven stepchildren), were certainly among these new recruits. Not a single one of
our mothers had worked outside the home, and they
had collectively experienced a modest six marriages
and sixteen children.

The explosion of women into the labor force is one
of the most important phenomena of the twentieth
century. Its impact goes well beyond the economic
indicators; it determines the way we live now, from
the time at which we must rise in the morning to the
way in which our after-work evenings and weekends
are spent. It affects the kind of food we eat, the magazines we read, the way we raise our children. But, as
with most important historical phenomena, those living
through it have a hard time explaining it.

There is a vague consensus among those whose life-
work it is to study the economy that more women in
the work force is a good thing for America. *Business
Week*, not known for its feminist tendencies, reported
in a 1984 cover story:

> The great American job machine is fast becoming the
> eighth wonder of the world. While employment has de-

clined in most industrial countries, the U.S. is creating jobs at breakneck speed—20 million in the past 10 years. Many experts seem baffled by this phenomenon but the reason is simple—women. . . . Because a rapidly expanding labor force is a principal element in propelling an economy onto a fast-growth track, the influx of women into the job market may be the major reason that the U.S. has emerged so much healthier than other countries from the economic shocks of the 1970's.[2]

According to *Business Week*, women have buoyed up the slumping economy in two ways. Their entry has been mainly into the loosely defined service sector, which includes a wide range of jobs from grocery-store checker to information processor. This has helped to promote an expanded service/information economy, which has compensated for a faltering manufacturing economy. Working women also have more money to spend, and they spend it. In addition to the clothes, lunches, and transportation that stepping out into the labor force requires, a married woman's income allows the family to buy the big-ticket items, like homes and cars.

This cheerful view of women working is from the cool eye of the economist. It says nothing about the long hours for low pay at work and the long hours of unpaid domestic labor after work that have gone into this economic salvation. According to a recent survey in *Ms.* magazine, women on the average put in 38.4 hours on the job and 24.8 hours at home for a total of 63.2 hours each week. Men put in 42.6 hours on the job but only 12.6 hours at home for a total work week of 54.2 hours.[3]

Surely women did not take on this heavy load for the patriotic purpose of saving the economy. Have they all bought the egalitarian ideal of the women's movement that the highest goal for women is to compete with men in the marketplace, not to hang around the kitchen or push the stroller?

The women's movement has diverted the attention of the media to women at the top, those who live to work, obscuring an understanding of what is happening to the great majority of women who are not at the top, and masking the larger economic forces that drive women's lives.

The women's movement which came of age in the seventies is riding on the crest of a greater wave. The economy does not need more women doctors, lawyers, and executives. It needs more secretaries, waitresses, and saleswomen. But as long as there is general growth in the service sector there is a little more room at the top of that sector also.

Much of the egalitarian message of the women's movement fits the need for female workers. The glorification of work outside the home and the devaluation of housework and motherhood help to push women into the work force. Delayed marriage and divorce force many women into the labor fold. By focusing on the few at the top in male occupations the women's movement does not threaten the low-wage structure of the female occupations. And by women's insisting on being treated as men are treated, no special expensive family support systems are required.

WOMEN WHO LIVE TO WORK

Women who live to work are the darlings of the Egalitarian Revolution. These are the women whose chief motivation is status rather than money. This does not mean that the women who live to work do not need money. Given the epidemic of divorce, the large percentage of single women in this category, and the shrinking wages of men, money is a compelling factor, but status is the driving force. The egalitarian message insists that women become scientists, not scientific technicians, even though a scientist's pay may not be much higher than a technician's and the training period, work load, and stress are much greater.

Women who live to work are convinced that equality means competing with men for men's jobs. They are flooding into law schools, medical schools, and M.B.A. programs to prepare themselves to grab power and status in the male world.

These are the women who saw their fathers or their friends' fathers march off to jobs that seemed glamorous: an office with a secretary, lunches in the city, important talk on the telephone, and important papers in leather briefcases. These women's mothers stayed home in a world that seemed dull, perhaps because it was too familiar. Now they have chosen to become their fathers, not realizing that they must be their mothers as well.

My classmates and I certainly responded to the egalitarian call. We are the kind of women—bright, ambitious, middle-class—who twenty years earlier would have found our status through our husbands. Then it would have been a social embarrassment if we had worked outside the home, revealing that our husbands could not adequately support us. But we would have been presidents of the PTA or leaders of the polio drive. Our energies and talents would have found some outlet, probably in the now degraded world of volunteerism.

Fifty years earlier, in the heyday of the suffrage campaign, we would have led the marches. In that era a few of us would have taken the difficult route of career, probably in medicine or academia, but we would have considered a career a dedication that precluded marriage or children.

Why at this time in history has there been an unprecedented call to take up male careers, and an unprecedented response? The ideological struggles of the sixties which focused first on blacks and later on women occurred in a period of rapid economic growth. The same call to compete with men for permanent positions in the job market would have been futile in the jobless thirties and unpatriotic in the wartime forties. The great American job machine, at least for a time, had openings at the top, the middle, and the bottom. And egalitarian ideology helped feed this machine.

The modern women's movement has put almost all its effort into creating and promoting women who live to work. It has romanticized the male status jobs and taken the position that systematic discrimination is the only reason that men rather than women hold these status jobs. Enforcement of Title VII and the pursuit of an Equal Rights Amendment have been adopted as the major strategies, on the assumption that if women could have an equal opportunity to compete with men they would win the race at least as often as men.

Title VII, originally drafted for blacks, dictates that women as well as racial and ethnic minorities must be given the opportunity to compete equally with white men in the marketplace. This strategy has worked well for some women who live to work, particularly women without children. But it has brought grief to many others. Even with superhuman effort, few medical residents, new lawyers, or executives with children at home can keep the same hours as their male counterparts.

At the top are the superwomen who definitely have made it—women like Geraldine Ferraro or Sandra Day O'Connor who have, to the public eye, grabbed the top male status jobs while gracefully maintaining a full family life. But most women who have taken on men's jobs have found it tough going. The rules have not changed to accommodate women, and indeed women have not asked to change the rules.

Overall, the results of the big push to place women in men's jobs have been disappointing. The number of women entering certain prestigious professions increased significantly between 1962 and 1978: physicians from 6 to 15 percent, lawyers from 4 to 15 percent, and engineers from one to 6 percent.[4] But the larger numbers of women entering the not-so-prestigious female occupations have eclipsed this advance. Two-thirds of women workers still enter female occupations.

WOMEN WHO WORK TO LIVE

The vast majority of women who entered the job market in the seventies and eighties did so because they needed the money, and the jobs were available. In a 1984 survey in *Ms.* (a magazine noted for its feminist readership), 58 percent of women surveyed said they took jobs "in order to make ends meet," 29 percent said they looked for work to achieve "a sense of accomplishment," and 11 percent to find out "what the outside world is all about."[5]

Women who work to live are for the most part marching to the beat of a different drum from women who live to work. The glorification of work promoted by the women's movement is viewed with suspicion. Most of their fathers did not commute to glamorous jobs in the city; they worked at dull jobs in factories or offices in order to support the family. They were often too tired in the evening to talk about anything—

certainly not their jobs. Their mothers considered marriage a liberation from work and were resentful if they had to return to work to make ends meet.

Their drummer is economic necessity. Two-thirds of all women in the labor force either are supporting themselves and their families or are married to men earning less than $15,000 a year.[6] Not only has divorce forced millions of women into the role of sole breadwinner, but married women have found that a rapidly changing economic structure means that a middle-class wage is now earned by two people.

In 1955 my father, then a midlevel civil servant, earned a salary which allowed him to support a nonworking wife and a child, own a modest home with a small mortgage, and drive an average-sized American car without a car loan. Even though the salaries of federal civil servants have improved relative to the private sector, a midlevel civil servant today could not afford to own that home and car and support a family on one salary in California, New York, and most urban areas across the country. The real downward spiral in middle-class wages began in the early seventies, as industrial productivity began to falter and then fall. The average forty-year-old man earned $28,100 in 1973 (in 1984 dollars) and only $24,600 in 1984, a drop of 13 percent.[7]

The American dream of owning your own home is now a two-person reality. The egalitarian call has soothed the pride of the husband who can no longer support his family even more than it has seduced women into the work force. Women as well as men are now expected to be breadwinners.

For the woman who is now the single head of household the situation is desperate. Her salary in the expanded service sector brings in only about 59 cents to the average dollar earned by men (a lower percentage relative to men than women in the male-dominated professions earn). Not only will this not begin to buy the house, it will not even pay the rent in many cities. These are the women who are working as hard as they can but are still falling into poverty.

For the young woman who has not yet married (the age of first marriage has been increasingly delayed), or who has already married and divorced, economic necessity often forces a move back to the parental home—a situation not welcomed by either generation. It is becoming a bitter joke that children never leave home anymore.

Women who work to live may find some status and satisfaction in their work, but they are not trying to capture the high status of male-dominated professions. Most women are entering fields that are already female-dominated or are fast becoming so. At the top end are the traditional female professions of teaching, nursing, and social work; at the bottom end, unskilled and semi-skilled manufacturing jobs. But the great middle bulge, where most of the new jobs have appeared, is the amorphous service sector.

The service sector is made up of many jobs, with secretarial, clerical, and now word processing as the largest components. All of these jobs demand communication and sometimes technical skills. They depend upon relatively well-educated labor and could not make use of the foreign-speaking immigrant labor that fueled America's manufacturing growth. They rarely demand the physical strength that was required to build our railways and dig our mines; they require instead the ability to talk to people.

Until recently the strategies of the women's movement completely ignored the great majority of working women who were simply working to live. Title VII is not helpful, since there are few if any males in these jobs with whom to achieve equality, and usually no upward career path in female-dominated occupations. Affirmative action is pointless in these occupations, since women are already overrepresented. Equal pay for equal work has no clout in occupations where only women are performing the tasks. And the failure to push for reliable publicly supported child care has kept millions of women in female occupations.

The recommendation of the women's movement was to get out of these occupations and find men's work. Don't become a nurse, become a doctor; forget about being a meter maid, go for policewoman. Only recently, with comparable worth, has the women's movement attempted to raise the pay of women in female-dominated professions without forcing women to leave them.

PART-TIME WORKERS

Big-picture statistics are often misleading. Although the majority of adult women work, only 43 percent work full time, year round[8] (as compared with 68 percent of men). The commonly accepted wisdom is that women work part time for "pin money," the little extra to buy new clothes or a family vacation. Although many women choose part-time work because they find it congenial with family life, some of the poorest women are forced into part-time work because they cannot find full-time work or cannot find adequate child-care arrangements to permit full-time work. These include the growing number of women who head single-parent households.

Part-time workers are not competing with men for status jobs. For the most part they are holding on to the fringe of the labor force with no security and no

benefits. Employers are now forced to pay Social Security for part-time workers, but such workers are
generally exempted from private retirement funds, from
health insurance, and from any seniority rights.
Part-time workers are found in all the occupations
populated by women who work to live, from teacher to
domestic worker. Part-time salaries, however, are rarely
proportionate to those for full-time jobs. A substitute
teacher or a part-time secretary must take an hourly
wage which is usually far below the rate paid to the
regular staff.

This huge group of workers has traditionally been
ignored by unions, by protective legislation, and certainly by the egalitarian strategies of the women's
movement.

REENTRY WOMEN

Reentry women are, by definition, women who have
left the job market for a significant period of time,
usually to raise children. They may return to work for
many reasons: divorce, widowhood, economic necessity
in marriage, college and graduate education for children, or simply to have something to do outside the
home. Some of these women have been influenced by
the egalitarian rhetoric of the women's movement, but
are realistic enough to realize that they cannot now
begin the competitive race with men. They will not, at
age forty-five, become brain surgeons or astronauts.
They do hope to get meaningful work and decent
pay.

What they all have in common are rusty skills, or no
skills at all, and a lack of self-confidence. A B.A. in
English circa 1960 does not thrill employment agencies

in the late 1980s. Traditional academic and training programs make little allowance for older students who are not hobbyists, and few older students can spend years retraining for employment.

These women are a great economic resource. They are at a time in their lives when they are not hindered by child care, and yet they still have great motivation and energy. Most of them are able and willing to work full time. Their homemaking experience has made them reliable and organized in a way many of them were not at twenty.

And yet these women are ignored by the women's movement, since, with their late start, they are quite unlikely to win the race for power. They will be forced to take the dregs of the job market for lack of direction and support. They will feel fortunate to be offered a job at all, and will work at menial tasks far below their competence and previous training.

PROFILE OF THE WOMAN WORKER

The most striking aspect of the current profile of women at work is that, except for the increased bulge in the number of women who are working to live, it is generally the same profile which existed in 1950. With a few small changes women are still clustered in a very narrow range of "female" occupations: secretarial work, retail sales, bookkeeping, private-household work, elementary-school teaching, waitressing, typing, cashiering, sewing and stitching, and nursing account for the jobs of a full two-fifths of all employed women. Sex segregation has actually increased over the past thirty years; for instance, 30 percent of all working women in 1960 held clerical jobs, but by 1979 the percentage of women workers in similar positions had increased to 35 percent.[9]

The crusade for equality in the marketplace has had little effect on the big picture of job distribution. Women who are working to live choose the jobs that are available to them, which are usually the ones that have traditionally been open to them. A few women have chosen jobs in the male-dominated world that either were not available twenty years ago or they would have considered inappropriate with family life, or both. But for every woman who becomes a lawyer ten women become secretaries, and the ratio remains the same.

What has changed is the acceptance of married women working. A 1960 public-opinion poll indicated that 34 percent of those interviewed approved of married women working; by 1978 approval had jumped to 70 percent, with over 80 percent of the under-thirties in agreement.[10] This kind of survey indicates a qualified approval. If the question were whether married women should have "careers," not jobs, the response would probably be less approving.

Many feminists claim credit for the public acceptance of married women working outside the home. While the feminist call for the independence of women through work complements the need of the economy for more women workers, the economic prerogatives of the country are the prime dictators of public opinion, as they always have been. Most people considered it immoral for married women to work during the Depression of the thirties. The few jobs available were reserved for the male breadwinners. By 1939 the hiring of married women had been banned by 84 percent of all U.S. insurance companies, 43 percent of public utilities, 29 percent of manufacturing concerns, and 23 percent of small businesses.[11] Then the voracious ap-

petite of the war production machine and the loss of
male labor to the military abruptly turned around public opinion. In 1937 working wives were denounced
in public-opinion polls, while only five years later 60
percent of people polled agreed that married women
should take jobs in war industries and another 24 percent approved of married women working under certain
conditions.[12]

Most women worked in manufacturing jobs during
World War II, jobs that had previously been held by
men. Rosie was riveting an airplane wing, not taking
dictation. These were the jobs that the G.I.s wanted
back when they returned home. Public opinion then
decided it was unpatriotic for women to hold these
male jobs, and in most cases there was no choice, since
women were promptly fired after V-J Day.

The expansion of the service sector after World War
II required more workers in traditional female occupations—jobs that had not been previously held by men.
Since there were not enough single women to fill the
slots, it became necessary to recruit married women
once again. Even in the fifties, the era which historians
insist glorified the suburban homemaker, there was a
rising swell of married women taking jobs in service
industries, but without widespread public acceptance.
By the seventies the imperatives of the economy required ever more women workers. Conveniently, the
women's movement helped persuade the public that it
was in fact a good thing for women to work outside the
home.

HOUSEWIVES

Mothers leaving the home to take their place in the
labor force have received a good deal of attention and

increasing public approval, overshadowing the 46 percent of all women between twenty-five and sixty who
remain in the home.[13] The major effect of the egalitarian crusade on these women at home is that they
now view themselves as "just a housewife." There is no
question that the attention the media has devoted to
the women who live to work has devalued the status
of those married women who work only in the home.
For most of the twentieth century not having to work
outside the home was considered prestigious, the mark
of having achieved middle-class status; now the prestige
is reserved for women who make it in the male world.

Married women remain at home for many reasons,
but the imperative of child care is certainly primary.
Even for families where the extra income is badly
needed, adequate child care which does not cost more
than the mother's salary is often not available. Some
families have chosen to sacrifice the needed income in
order to keep Mother at home. And in a minority of
families the father's income is more than adequate and
a second income is not required.

Many women remain at home after the children are
gone, and a few who have no children do so also. Presumably for these women economic necessity and their
diminished status as homemakers are not critical issues.

Women carrying the egalitarian standard have a difficult time with the traditional full-time housewife,
since this is the role they are specifically rejecting.
While work outside the home is seen as meaningful
and glamorous, work inside the home is viewed as demeaning and worthless. In this vision, no attempt is
made to separate child care from washing the dishes.

Betty Friedan, who allegedly created the housewives'
revolt, coined the phrase "the problem that has no
name" in 1963 to describe the desperate discontent that
she perceived was felt by educated women who were

devoting themselves to their home and family. "I love the kids and Bob and my home. There's no problem you can even put a name to. But I am desperate. I begin to feel I have no personality. I'm a server of food and putter-on of pants and a bedmaker, somebody who can be called on when you want something. But who am I?"[14]

For many women, the route to liberation from domestic drudgery was liberation from the family. The only chance for true equality with men lay outside the patriarchal family structure. Others, like Jessie Bernard in *The Future of Marriage*, held out the utopian vision that the housewife role would be abolished when men and women shared equally the responsibilities of work in the home and outside the home.[15]

In the real world of the seventies full-time housewives were ending their careers on the rocks of divorce in astonishing numbers. Divorce put a new light on housework: how much is it worth in dividing marriage assets? Faced with the massive divorce crisis, some women's organization, most notably NOW, attempted to solve the problem by assigning a dollar value to housework. Other groups suggested that housewives be paid an actual wage by their husbands while still married, to give their work the status of paid labor.[16]

The problem with this approach is that housework alone has a relatively low value in the labor market. It is usually performed by unskilled women who are not organized and who command the lowest wages. The Social Security Administration in 1976 estimated the annual value of a housewife's work at $4,705.[17] This low figure would be harmful rather than helpful to most women in a divorce settlement, and would do nothing to raise their status vis-à-vis a husband who earned $40,000 a year.

The most important service that housewives perform

is the care and attention to children twenty-four hours a day. Live-in child care can be purchased on the labor market at a price beyond all but a few families. The affection and concern of a parent cannot be purchased at all. It is wrongheaded for critics of housework to include child care as another category of housework along with doing the laundry. While it is possible to ignore the laundry for days or even a week, it is not possible to ignore a crying baby for more than a few minutes, or a sick or hungry child.

The market also does not measure the value of the housewife as a discriminating consumer. The consumer economy requires an ever greater attention to the selecting, buying, and servicing of commodities. In the pre-consumer era the housewife made the bread and toasted the bread on the fire, which she also made, after chopping the wood. Except for buying a winter's worth of flour, she may never have had to leave her home. In the consumer era, the housewife must choose a toaster among many competing brands at a store, she must shop for and choose the kind of bread that she toasts in the toaster, when the toaster breaks she must leave her home to have the toaster repaired. All these activities require discrimination and take time. These tasks are described by philosopher Ivan Illich as "shadow work."

When feminists argue that women should be paid for what they do to ready for consumption what the family income buys, they are mistaken when they ask for wages. The best they can hope for is not a shadow price but a consolation prize. The gratis performance of shadow work is the single most fundamental condition for the family's dependence on commodities. Even if these commodities were to be produced increasingly by robots, industrial society could not function without shadow work.[18]

Ultimately, the value of homemaking depends not upon its labor value in the marketplace, or upon the value of "shadow work" in a consumer society, but upon the status that it holds in society.

The egalitarian crusade pushed housewives far down the status ladder, but they are likely to make a strong comeback. It is dawning on women that working outside the home is not a choice but a necessity. "The problem that has no name" now has a name; it is fatigue. Choosing to stay at home has become a luxury that few families can afford, and, like any luxury, it will acquire the golden aura of high status.

5

WHY WOMEN EARN BOTTOM DOLLAR

When a man explicitly vows to the Lord, the equivalent for a human being, the following scale shall apply: if it is a male from twenty to sixty years of age, the equivalent is fifty shekels of silver by the sanctuary weight: if it is a female, the equivalent is thirty shekels.

—LEVITICUS 27:2–4

So proclaimed the Old Testament three thousand years ago. Presumably the ancient Israelis were discussing the relative values of men and women as slaves, but modern American women will recognize the depressingly familiar ratio. The most consistent generalization about women in the labor force is that women earn, on the average, about sixty cents to every dollar earned by men and have done so since 1920.[1] Recently it was announced that the ratio for full-time women workers had broken an important barrier and is now seventy cents to the male dollar.[2] This may indicate an important trend, a temporary cyclical upswing, or it may simply indicate that male wages are declining with the slumping manufacturing sector. It may be that women's real wages are not going up but men's wages are coming down.

The wage gap democratically includes women who work to live and women who live to work, women who scrub floors and women in executive management. The ratio fluctuates over time and varies somewhat among occupations and between black and white women, but it has shown little sign of budging under the onslaught of egalitarian strategies. In fact, demographer Gordon Green has found that the wages of white women entering the job market were three percentage points further behind comparable men in 1980 than they were in 1970.[3]

But these comparisons of the relative wages of women and men do not take into account the part-time worker, which is the pattern of most women workers. Part-time work is usually paid at a lower rate than full-time, and would further widen this wage gap if counted.

Women fare worse in America, the golden land of opportunity, than they do in other industrialized nations, which their ancestors left behind to improve their situation. In Italy women's wages in 1982 were 86 percent of men's, in Denmark 86 percent, in France 78 percent, in Sweden 74 percent, in West Germany, 73 percent.[4]

And the wage gap persists in spite of the fact that women are generally better educated than men who hold similar jobs. Barely half of the white males in white-collar jobs have completed four years of high school or more, while three-quarters of women have done so.[5]

There are many theories to explain why women make up the poorly paid underbelly of the American labor force. These range from a universal male conspiracy to achieve female subordination, to lower productivity and less consistent commitment on the part of women workers. A current popular explanation is the "crowding" theory. This theory (which encompasses several others) argues that women are allowed to enter relatively few occupations, where their wages are kept artificially low because there are so many more women available for their positions.[6] Depending upon your ideological stance, it may be the impersonal marketplace which holds the door closed to other occupations, or it may be a conscious choice made by men to keep women out. The women's movement holds that it is discrimination by males that holds the doors closed. If the law forces the doors open to higher-paid male occupations, women will rush in and grab the higher-paying jobs.

But this theory has not held up with the new wave of women who have entered male professions. They also earn about three-fifths of what men earn in these professions. Between 1960 and 1980 the percentage of women managers rose from 14.5 percent to 28 percent, while the gap between the earnings of male managers and female managers widened from 58 percent to 55 percent.[7]

The explanation of the wage gap is not simple discrimination. Although discrimination has certainly played a role in the jobs women hold, it has not been the most important factor. Most women choose jobs that will accommodate the demands of children and family. Young women who have no children or who are not yet married still consider this the strongest determinant in their occupational choice. Even women who live to work must eventually find niches in their male-dominated professions which will accommodate their family obligations—usually at lower pay.

Women with children choose jobs in which they have *control over their time* and in which they can *conserve their energy*. They must have jobs with a very regular schedule, within a reasonable distance of their home, and that require no unexpected evening or weekend overtime. They must be able to call in sick when their child is sick, and they must be able to leave the job market for fairly long periods when necessary and then return to it. They must also hold jobs that are not so physically or mentally stressful that they have no energy left for their family.

And for women with small children (60 percent of whom are now in the labor force[8]), the single most important determinant of where they work, how long they work, and what kind of work they perform is *reliable child care.*

Two of the occupations where women work in large numbers today, as they have done for the past sixty years, are elementary-school teaching and secretarial work. These jobs are criticized by the women's movement as being extensions of the stereotypical female roles of mother/nurturer of little children and wife/subordinate of husband. Systematic discrimination, it is asserted, has barred women from the higher-status, higher-paying jobs of school administrator and executive respectively.

An elementary-school teacher has good control over her time. She can return home when her children return home, and she can share vacations with her children. To become a school administrator at higher pay entails longer hours and often work over the summer vacation;

but until very recently only a small percentage of married women worked outside the home. In the seventeenth and eighteenth centuries, in addition to cleaning, cooking, and caring for their children, colonial women routinely engaged in household manufacture. They spun, wove, and made lace, soap, shoes, and candles which were sold to merchants. On the frontier, women pitched in with the farmwork and developed home industries of tailoring and washing for those farmers without wives. With all of this very hard work, women still controlled their own time and determined their own expenditure of energy. Men, of course, did so as well. When men entered the industrial wage system and adopted its timetable and pace, they had to relinquish their domestic responsibilities.

Clearly it is not possible to return to cottage industry, but it is possible to recognize and accept that women today have the same need to control their time and conserve their energy as they did in the seventeenth century. Male occupations will be ill-suited to women with children unless they are modified to accommodate these criteria.

The absence or presence of child care for women with small children is the number-one determinant of whether they work at all, whether they work part time or full time, and what kind of work they perform.

The theory of systematic and purposeful sex discrimination does not allow for the very real needs of women to control their time and energy; it also does not recognize the critical role of child care.

The absence of reliable child care is both a source of anguish for working mothers and an effective bar to working in many occupations or to working full time. Male-dominated professions where workers have little control over their own time become impossible for women who must live by the timetable of baby-sitting arrangements. The flexibility of part-time work, at much lower pay with few benefits, is often the only choice.

All mothers, whether they live to work or work to live, suffer the nightmare of child care, which is universally in short supply and all too often low in quality. Shockingly, we are the only industrialized nation that has no national policy on maternity leave. The minimum paid leave among the other more industrialized countries is twelve weeks, while the most frequent pattern among European countries is five months.[10] Our Supreme Court has recently decreed that it is constitutional for California to give four months *unpaid* leave,[11] but that it is also all right for the other states to offer nothing if they so choose.

It is perplexing that a country whose current buoyant economy has grown on the backs of working women has provided no child-care support to attract and keep them in the working force. The statistics are awesome and the trend is growing; 60 percent of women with children under three are in the work force, and 49 percent of married women with infants under one year of age work outside the home.[12] But child-care needs do not stop at age five. According to congressional testimony, up to fifteen million children ages five to thirteen care for themselves, often in empty homes, while both their parents or their only parent is at work.[13]

The explanation for our negligent lack of policy and support is that there has been no cohesive push for it. An English woman lawyer who had spent nearly a year in America said to me, "It is amazing what you Americans put up with, and you are such a rich country." She was referring to the general inadequacy of our social-support systems, including health and child care.

The women's movement has given child care casual attention but has not made the issue a priority. Al-

though it is obvious that women need child care if they
are going to compete with men in the marketplace, asking for a public solution is asking for a special favor,
not equal treatment. The Equal Rights Amendment,
which attracted the full attention and resources of the
women's movement, pushed in the opposite direction
from the special concerns of women as mothers by insisting that women be treated as men are treated. Men
have not demanded a national policy on child care;
they consider child care a woman's problem.

The women's movement has implicitly accepted the
American "myth of the self-sufficient family," as it has
been labeled by the Carnegie Council for Children.[14]
This myth, which preceded the women's movement,
issues from the American spirit of rugged individualism
and holds that the family that is not on public assistance does not want and does not need public support;
the state must not interfere with the private arrangements within a family except for three areas that have
been historically carved out: compulsory education,
state control of marriage and divorce procedures, and
state supervision of families on public assistance.

In all eras of American history many families did
without critical medical and other forms of social support. But this myth of the self-sufficient family has
broken down irretrievably under the burden of massive
divorce and the needs of unprecedented numbers of
mothers returning to work.

And yet feminists have clung to the myth and have
fitted it to their egalitarian vision that the family will
remain private and self-sufficient but will adapt to the
new equal partnership of working parents by equally
distributing household and child care between husband
and wife, with minimal outside help. This simply builds
one myth upon another. Although it is quite feasible
for two working adults without children to share the

minimal household chores required to maintain a couple, the only way that child care can be shared equally is if each partner has a part-time job. There are very few circumstances (except perhaps university teaching, or families wealthy enough to afford full-time help) where both adults can maintain full jobs without outside child care.

The egalitarian vision fails at almost every level. For whatever reason, in the United States, and in other countries where emphasis has been placed on equal parental responsibility (including Sweden), women still bear by far the greater burden of child care. But in the United States women must find private solutions to what should be a public problem.

Women cope by luck or money, and often there is not enough of either. Dr. Sheila Kamerman, who investigated two hundred white and black families in Westchester County, New York, with at least one child under five, claims that their children "may experience three, four, or even more kinds of care in an average week, as they spend a part of the day in nursery school, another part with a family day-care mother (or two different such women) and are brought to and from these services by a parent, a neighbor, or some other person."[15] Across the nation, mothers panic when a child wakes in the night with a stomachache, or when a home-care mother says she is taking a family vacation. The fragile structure of support that mothers must weave can be broken by any number of mundane incidents.

The American government's involvement with day care has been limited in the past to national emergencies and recently to the prevailing poverty policy.

The largest federal day-care programs were responses to the Depression and World War II. In the 1930s, under Franklin D. Roosevelt, places for about forty thousand children were set up in day nurseries under the Works Projects Administration. The main purpose of these nurseries was not to provide enrichment for the children or relief for their working mothers, but to provide jobs for teachers, nurses, nutritionists and maintenance workers who would have been otherwise unemployed. When World War II effectively ended the Depression, the WPA nurseries were phased out, but even larger federal day nurseries were set up, this time to accommodate the war-worker mothers, not the nursery-school teachers. Under the Lanham Act, 1.5 million places were created for children; they were abolished when the war ended and the mothers were sent home from the defense plants.[16]

The relationship of day care to poverty began in the latter half of the nineteenth century when millions of poor immigrants flooded into large cities. Upper-class women who were concerned about their welfare set up day nurseries as a response to "the plight of small, dirty, ill-behaved lower-class children who were left alone daily."[17]

Day care for the poor was dropped for most of the twentieth century. It was picked up again in the war against poverty in the sixties and was seen as the unfortunate solution for people who could not look after themselves. As the Children's Bureau of the Department of Health, Education and Welfare declared in 1963, "The child who needs day care has a family problem which makes it impossible for his parents to fulfill their parental responsibilities without supplementary help."[18] Head Start, the popular nursery-school program for the cultural enrichment of disadvantaged children, and day-care subsidies for mothers receiving Aid for Families with Dependent Children, AFDC, were the main beneficiaries of congressional concern.

During the early seventies there were several congressional attempts to extricate day care from poverty and to provide a general solution for all working mothers. The Comprehensive Child Development Act of 1971 broke the tie between poverty and child care and provided a sliding scale for all, including middle-class parents. This bill passed Congress, but was vetoed by President Nixon, who explicitly stated that it undermined the American family: "For the federal Government to plunge headlong financially into supporting child development would commit the vast moral authority of the National Government to the side of communal approaches to child rearing over against the family-centered approach."[19]

Nixon's concern about "communal approaches to child rearing" betrays an underlying belief that communal child care is closely related to communism: this is the kind of thing Russia does, while American families take care of their own children.

Several other watered-down congressional attempts failed in the seventies, and the federal government began shifting more responsibility for social services to the state governments, enforcing a ceiling on federal contributions to any state's day-care programs. This trend toward getting out of the social-service business accelerated under the Reagan Administration.

Leaving child care to the states has meant leaving it to a hodgepodge of licensing systems, a free-for-all of for-profit day-care franchises, and a general low level of care. Most child care is now in the private for-profit sector, and the picture is not rosy. A 1972 national study rated only 15 percent of the for-profit centers as good or superior, while 38 percent of the public and private nonprofit centers were given that rating; fully 50 percent of the profit-oriented centers were rated as poor, as compared with 11 percent of the nonprofit centers.[20] There is no reason to suspect that the crush of children who have joined the day-care ranks since 1972 has improved the situation.

Ironically, the attitudes of our heads of state regarding the sanctity of the full-time mother for raising children has not been matched by the baby experts. Advice on raising children is a notoriously flexible business which tends to bend with historical trends. Maxine Margolis in her work on changing attitudes toward American women, *Mothers and Such*, demonstrates how expert opinion nearly turned itself on its head between World War II and the eighties. Dr. Benjamin Spock, the reigning baby doctor of the postwar maternity boom, advocated permissive baby-raising, which meant that the mother must respond to the baby's schedule, making motherhood an even more demanding job than it already was. Employment outside the home was taboo:

> . . . useful, well-adjusted citizens are the most valuable possessions a country has, and good mother care during early childhood is the surest way to produce them. . . . If a mother realizes clearly how vital this kind of care is to a small child, it may make it easier for her to decide that the extra money she might earn, or the satisfaction she might receive from an outside job, is not so important after all.[21]

Child experts eventually responded to the changing times. The turning point was 1972, when for the first time more mothers of school-age children were in the labor force than were at home. Even Dr. Spock changed his tune in his 1976 edition, with a new chapter on working families in which he asserted: "Parents who know they need a career or a certain kind of work for fulfillment should not simply give it up for their children." He suggested that these parents "work out some kind of compromise between their two jobs and the needs of their children, usually with the help of other caregivers."[22]

Mother was not so all-important after all; fathers and even non-family members might be enlisted into Baby's world. Prominent psychologist Jerome Kagan stated that the notion that a child can form only a single attachment is "like saying a person can only love one other person. And that's nonsense."[23]

Day care was examined anew, and the old studies which predicted that institutionalized babies would be developmentally stunted were discredited. Day care now was thought to offer a positive developmental advantage. The smothering nature of the exclusive mother–child relationship would be mitigated by the influence of others. Emphasis was placed on the long historical tradition of several adults looking after several children, as opposed to the very brief historical moment when it was only the mother who did this.

However, all of the experts' newfound confidence depends on "good" day care. Although the standards for what constitutes "good" day care are not clear, there is a consensus on what makes for bad day care: too few adults for too many children, a passive environment in which the TV is the center of attention, too little individual attention and affection, unreliability, and lack of flexibility. Unfortunately this is what many desperate mothers must settle for.

As a nation we seem to have resigned ourselves to making do with individual solutions, rather than establishing a uniform national policy. In a 1985 *New York Times* editorial entitled "Who's Watching the Kids?" the editor described a bill before Congress intended to beef up existing day-care facilities, primarily for low-income families. His conclusion, which could stand as a representative statement of the prevailing "hodgepodge" approach: "Different families have different needs, and child care always has to remain a hodgepodge. But each component ought to be the best that can be devised."[24]

The most recent tactic is to twist the arms of corporations to provide child care. An optimistic study published by the Conference Board in New York claimed that 1,800 companies are now providing child-care assistance, ranging from a day-care center at work to an information and referral service.[25] A long-term legislative study of the crisis of child care in California also reached the conclusion that it should become the responsibility of corporate employers.

The corporate approach is simply ducking the issue. It is as if we insisted that our employers, not the government, should voluntarily assume the education of our children. Although some employers might do a good job of it, many would refuse and others would offer cheap solutions. Also, many women are self-employed or work for employers far too small to offer such benefits. We would not accept a hodgepodge approach to our children's education.

As part of a major rethinking of national family law and policy, child care must receive a top priority. We have the example of all the other Western industrialized countries to learn from. Although none of them completely satisfies the growing demand for child care (France provides the most comprehensive care), all of them have taken the position that child care, like public education, is for everyone, not just mothers on welfare; parents can, of course, make their own private arrangements if they choose, but the state will provide good quality care at fair rates.

Sweden is often looked to as a shining light, since it has the most developed and oldest policy of any West-

ern nation. Its comprehensive family-support system begins with intensive prenatal care, total coverage of childbirth, and good postnatal care for mothers and babies.
Sweden rates among the highest in the world for infant
health, and among the lowest for infant mortality. America offers a dismal comparison, with 18 infant deaths
per 1,000 to Sweden's 10 per 1,000.[26]

One of the most intriguing features of the Swedish
family-support system is the parental-leave system. Every family, whether both parents are employed or not,
is given a nine-month allowance to help with the expenses generated by the new baby. If both parents are
employed they are also entitled to nine months' leave
of absence *between* them at 90 percent pay and an additional three months more at reduced pay. After the
parents return to work they are allowed a maximum of
sixty days per year for either one of them to stay home
with a sick child. Parents with children under the age
of eight may work a six-hour day rather than the traditional eight, but with a corresponding reduction in pay.[27]

The year-long parental-leave policy in Sweden is a
recognition that infant care presents special problems.
Not only is it physically and emotionally difficult to separate mother and child in the first year of life, it is very
expensive. According to the Yale Bush Center Advisory
Committee on Infant Care, it costs at least $5,200 per
year per baby in the United States to provide the minimum ratio of caretakers to babies (one to three). For
the average working mother, who brings home about
$8,000 after taxes, this is a discouraging margin. A pa-
rental-leave system which provides some income is the
best solution. Seventy-five nations have statutory provisions that guarantee infant-care leave of some kind. The
United States has none. (At this writing a bill to guarantee a four-month parental leave *without pay* is being

tossed about in Congress—a first step in the right direction, but useless for mothers whose income is critical for family survival.)

The United States must catch up with its poorer European cousins and offer a *paid* parental leave of at least six months to either parent. For the good and practical reasons discussed in Chapter One, the mother, as the parent who has given birth, will be the most likely recipient, but the income offered to either parent must be at least 50 percent of her or his salary (up to a certain limit). Highest-quality prenatal and postnatal care must be guaranteed, without regard to whether the parents are officially indigent. When the mother (or father) returns to work, a sick leave of at least two weeks each year, specifically for the care of sick children, must be offered.

Following the parental leave, child care for working mothers in the United States must be considered a responsibility of the society as a whole, as is reading and writing for children. Although this is a radical departure from the myth of the self-sufficient family, it suits the reality of a society which has come to depend upon the labor of its mothers outside the home.

Children require different kinds of care at different ages. Following the parental leave, up till the age of three a voucher based on a sliding scale of need could be given directly to the working mother. Public and private day-care and home-care facilities could receive the voucher, creating a free market. All child-care facilities would be carefully licensed, based on federal guidelines.

After the age of three it is possible to extend our public-education system to meet the needs of its constituents. The facilities and the teachers in this system could be expanded to include full-day preschool and day care for little children, beginning at age three, and after-school care for older children. Many school districts have empty schools or partially filled schools that could be converted to preschools. This idea was first conceived by the American Federation of Teachers in the late sixties, foreseeing the dwindling numbers of elementary-school children, but was aborted by Richard Nixon's veto of the Comprehensive Child Development Act in 1971.[28]

In fact, education in this country now routinely begins at age three or four for those who can afford it. A study from the National Center of Education shows that 53 percent of children aged three to four whose families had incomes of $25,000 and above attended a preschool program in 1982, while less than 29 percent of children whose families had incomes below $25,000 attended preschool.[29]

Preschool education pays off. Disadvantaged youngsters who are given quality preschool education through Head Start or other publicly funded programs do have a better life. Several studies have followed these children through young adulthood and found that they stay in school longer, have fewer teenage pregnancies, commit fewer crimes and earn higher incomes. One study, the Perry Preschool Project of Ypsilanti, Michigan, tried to put a dollar value on the gain to the community in terms of lower crime rates and greater tax contributions of the more than sixty poor black children they followed through their teen years. It calculated that their rate of return was seven times the cost of the program.[30]

After the age of five, the emphasis should be on adequate after-school and emergency or sick care. Most public schools already have facilities which are usually vacant after school hours. It is much less costly to supervise older children, since they do not need the same ratio of child to adult required by very young children.

The prevailing reality of "latchkey" children who go home to empty houses and often wait in fear until a parent returns is inexcusable. Girl Scouts and Boy Scouts have taken up the necessary task of teaching millions of children how to deal with strangers at the door and on the phone when they are home alone.[31]

There is no doubt that the needed services cost money. Quality preschool alone costs at least four thousand dollars each year per child. But the alternatives are even more expensive. A generation of children that are raised in a hodgepodge of care arrangements that only the lucky and the rich can escape does not bode well for the future of the country. For mothers who are heads of households, reliable child care can break the cycle of poverty and public dependency that costs a great deal more than the cost of child care. Ruth Sidell, in her thorough investigation of women and children in poverty, *Women and Children Last*, states: "There is little doubt that the absence of a high-quality, coherent comprehensive day-care policy is a key factor in the perpetuation of poverty among women and children."[32]

A comprehensive child-care policy must originate at the federal level. If left to the states alone, or to local governments, which for the most part is the current situation, it will continue to be hodgepodge, with excellent facilities in some locations and virtually no facilities in others. The federal government has the power of the pocketbook and can use it to set up strict licensing criteria.

Child care and preschool can be funded in many ways. For instance, the parental leave can be funded through a joint employee/employer/government insurance arrangement like Social Security. Unlike Social Security, there will not be a staggering balloon payment thirty years down the road. Child care before the age of three could be administered by this same insurance system, with a voucher payment, based on a sliding scale of need, given directly to the working parent, to be used in federally licensed facilities.

Preschool and after-school programs should be administered by the school district, with money and standards determined by the federal government. The critical question to be asked here is whether preschool and perhaps after-school care should be recognized as a free entitlement for all children regardless of need, as public schools are for all children from kindergarten through high school. In France, the *écoles maternelles*, free preschools for children from age three to six, have been well established since the 1950s and are attended by virtually all children, whether or not their mothers work.[33] Ultimately, this should be our national commitment (only 40 percent of the mothers of children under six do not work), since preschool education has proved to be a valuable learning and socialization experience for small children. But in the press of the present, a sliding scale based on need could be the interim solution, with the federal government picking up the difference.

Child care and other issues relating to family policy require a great deal of concerted pressure at the national, i.e., congressional, level. This should be an issue around which all working mothers should unite without regard to individual political persuasion. The same spirit that rallied millions of women of different backgrounds to fight for the ERA, which had no obvious practical application, should be resurrected to fight for an issue that would alleviate the everyday burden of most working women.

Child care is a problem whose time has come. The revolt of women workers will surely begin with this battle. But it is only the first battle in the war to raise wages for women. Ideal child-care arrangements would surely allow women to seek better jobs or to work full time rather than part time, but women will still have the need to control their time and to conserve their energy for the family they come home to. For these reasons women will still crowd the "female" occupations like word processing or teaching, which meet these needs.

If women choose or fall into occupations which best suit their needs for controlling time and energy, does it follow inevitably that these occupations must pay low wages? Does the Old Testament dictate of thirty shekels for women and fifty for men contain the essence of a universal law?

The American workplace is not a free market; it is studded with protected pockets created by unions, licenses, civil service, and tenure systems. Workers in these pockets enjoy a high degree of job security, and they carefully restrict new recruits. They use their exclusive status to demand higher wages and better working conditions. A gardener who works for the city and is a member of the union earns wages that are greater than he or she could earn outside the union. Professional associations for doctors and lawyers have set up highly restrictive licensing requirements that severely limit their numbers.

Most women work outside these protected pockets. They do not command the job security and the exclusive numbers that allow them to improve their wages or their conditions.

The wage gap is *not* immutable. Now that women have become a huge and permanent part of the labor force they have a real opportunity to organize and wipe away the wage gap. Imaginative tactics, combined with tight national and local organization, can accomplish this. A two-pronged approach is called for—one which both seeks to raise the wages and working conditions in

female-dominated professions and opens real job tracks
in male occupations that allow women better control
over their time and energy. (Specific strategies for specific groups will be discussed in the chapters on living
to work, on working to live, and on part-time and reentry women.)

6

WOMEN
WHO LIVE TO WORK

SUPERWOMEN

"I'm not going to pay you like a broad, and I'm not going to treat you like a broad, so don't act like a broad."[1] With this warning Karen Valenstein was hired into her first job as an investment banker. She has climbed to become the first vice-president at E. F. Hutton, where, at thirty-eight, she is one of the preeminent women in investment banking, with an annual salary in the range of a quarter of a million dollars plus bonuses.

Valenstein has not acted at all like a "broad" and has played a man's game better than most men. As reported in a cover story of *The New York Times Magazine*, this includes trading locker-room vulgarities and reciting National Football League scores on Monday morning. It also includes a punishing schedule. In two months she packed in five round trips to the West Coast, thirty-nine office meetings, twenty-six business-related meals, and twenty-one days that stretched from one sunrise to the next.[2] Valenstein plays the game to win. As the president of the Financial Women's Association of New York observed, "She is truly competitive in all the ways we need to succeed." Yet Valenstein has two young children, a husband of fourteen years and a life outside the office.

Clearly some women do appear to have it all. These are the superstars of the egalitarian revolution that have captured the male status jobs and still have a family to come home to. Thousands of women reading about Valenstein in the *Times Magazine* on that Sunday morning undoubtedly felt a mixture of envy and defeat as they compared her with their own inadequate performance of balancing career and children.

The women's movement has insisted that if women are given the chance to compete on an equal footing with men in the world of power and status they will get to the top, and some do. Are the Karen Valensteins just the tip of the iceberg of what will become a truly sexually integrated power structure?

A closer look into Valenstein's domestic life reveals at least one of the secrets of her success. In addition to a full-time housekeeper, her husband holds the nest together. He takes the children to school, supervises their activities, cooks their meals on the weekend, and builds them jungle gyms. He accepts his wife's grueling schedule and is rarely included in her entertaining. "What she does would kill me, particularly the nighttime stuff," says Mr. Valenstein.[3]

Extraordinary ambition and energy, full-time domestic help and an unusually supportive husband: this is the blueprint for achieving superwoman status. While men with families can make it to the top with a single traditional wife, women can do it only with costly outside help. This usually means also a husband who is supportive both emotionally and financially.

Geraldine Ferraro and Margaret Thatcher appear near the top of any list of the world's most famous women. They have achieved worldwide prominence through their own efforts, not their husbands', and yet a close look at their lives reveals a similar support system to that of Valenstein's.

Geraldine Ferraro, well known to the American public as a feisty, energetic woman, was also revealed, during an investigation of her financial disclosure, to be married to a man of considerable means. The media assault on the Ferraro-Zaccarro financial situation highlighted every decimal point of their assets.

What the media did not reveal, but what Ferraro made clear in her autobiography, *Ferraro: My Story,* was the incredible emotional as well as financial support her husband had provided throughout her career. He encouraged her to go to law school and, while the children were still in their teens, both encouraged and helped finance her campaign for Congress in 1978. With the help of a housekeeper, he manned the home fires, driving the children to and from school in Manhattan every day on his way to work, while she spent the week in Washington.

In spite of all my obligations, he never complained [she writes]. Not only that, but when I was making the political rounds in Queens, he would come with me from place to place, night after night without a word. At one point I was so exhausted that I said to him, "I just can't go tonight." That should have been music to his ears, but John always had my priorities straight.

John certainly didn't need to go, but he said, "Come on, Gerry. You've got to do it," he urged me. "Let's go." And he went.[4]

Margaret Thatcher, whose decisive style has impressed world leaders and prompted respect, if not always admiration, at home, is the daughter of a greengrocer. Through determination and intellect she crossed the formidable class and sex barriers of English life and attended aristocratic Oxford, where she studied chemistry. There she met and married the wealthy businessman Dennis Thatcher, who promoted and supported first her legal training as a barrister and then her career as member of Parliament and party leader. "He thought it would be a pity if all that talent were wasted," she remarked in a BBC interview.[5]

The Thatcher twins were born just before her final exam for barrister. Claiming she was very torn by the decision, she took her exam and resumed her legal career immediately, with the support of good household help. "I said to myself, 'If I am not careful, I am not going to get back to law or politics.'" When the children were six she became a member of Parliament and continued her march to the top. When asked how she managed the demands of career and family, Thatcher smiled and said, "Somehow women cope."

But women do not always cope. For many superwomen, the all-important support structure is fragile. "Wonder Woman Judge Whose Life Ended in Suicide" announced the bold headline of the *San Francisco Examiner*. The story related the sad fate of Karen Gunderson, a Nevada City judge who took her life in 1985 because she felt she had failed as a wife and mother. An extremely bright and ambitious young woman, she had served as a prosecuting attorney, a job which she had described in an earlier interview: "Being a prosecutor in a large city is a rough and tumble job. I put a lot of pressure on myself to be the best, to ease the way for women who would follow me. I felt I had to prove that women could do the job. I worked twice as hard and twice as long as any of the men."[6]

Gunderson waited until she was thirty-eight to have a baby. Her husband had promised to help her, since she was often awakened in the middle of the night to sign search warrants, but instead he left to marry another woman shortly after the baby was born. Apparently the next two years were agony for Gunderson, although the only complaint that she made to her co-workers was that she was always tired because the baby kept her awake at night.[7]

Gunderson's tragedy is not common, but the stress, conflict and just plain fatigue that overwhelmed her hits a sympathetic nerve in the thousands of women who live to work. Without the emotional and practical support of her husband she simply could not cope.

THE ALSO-RANS

Superwomen are a mixed blessing for women who live to work. Their rise to the top in male-dominated professions sets a precedent which makes the way easier for those who wish to follow in their paths. It is now far more possible in America for a woman to become vice-president or even president, because of the psychological barrier broken by Ferraro's candidacy. But superwomen also provide an unrealistic model which is not possible for most women with children to emulate. Most women who are seeking success in male-dominated occupations are not superwomen. They do not have that necessary combination of incredible ambition, enormous energy, and the twin support pillars of an unusually supportive husband and excellent household help that enable women with families to get to the top.

Women need more than equal opportunity with men to get to the top. Men with families in the high-stress, time-demanding fields of politics, law, and high finance do not require personal wealth to manage their home life. Their wives do. Since there are in fact fewer real househusbands than angels on the head of a rattle, it is virtually a requirement that women who work more than from nine to five, and who put a great deal of energy into their jobs, have very good household help; and this is always expensive. Even women who can afford household help have problems. In recent American history, the pool of reliable domestic workers has virtually dried up. Women who would have chosen domestic work or child care in earlier times now choose what they consider higher-status jobs as waitresses or clerks. Mothers must depend on an unreliable procession of illegal immigrants and transient workers. The continuous domestic crises that this produces could provide material for a TV sitcom, but they are rarely funny for the mothers who live through them.

The bottom line is that there are only so many hours in the day and children require the attention of at least one parent for some of those hours. Very few women who live to work can feel comfortable with household help filling all the children's hours.

Although women are entering some male-dominated professions, notably law, medicine, and middle management, in greater numbers than they have in the past (they are not entering technical fields in a higher proportion), it is the rare woman who climbs to the top. In Karen Valenstein's world, investment banking, there are many women in middle management, but almost none at her level. Catalyst, a New York–based research group, states that only eight out of every thousand employed women hold high-level executive, administrative, or managerial jobs, and women occupy only 3 percent of the seats on Fortune 500 corporate boards. Even more to the point, a recent Gallup Poll noted that 42 percent of high-level female executives surveyed were single, divorced, or separated, and that fewer than half have children.[8]

The central problem is that male occupations have made no accommodation to the needs of working mothers, and that women have asked for none. The egalitarian rhetoric of the past twenty years has forced women into working the same impossibly long hours with the same kind of tough aggressiveness as men. Women have not only had to compete with no special consideration, they have often felt obliged to play a man's game harder than a man plays it. And after a hard day's fight they must come home to children and domestic responsibilities.

Rather than attempting to change the work style of the career they have chosen, or accept the fact that family responsibilities will limit their career ambitions, women tend to blame themselves. "If only I were better organized or more energetic, I could be the senior vice-president, or the chief of staff," etc. In a New York Times op ed piece entitled "Women's Near Liberation" Kati Morton charges that women do not get to the top because they are not self-centered. "Women must learn to focus on their dreams at the expense of other, lesser commitments. Einstein was focused. So was Virginia Woolf. So is Meryl Streep."[9]

Rather than look at what they have achieved, women look at what they have not. The few superwomen who dot all high-status professions stand as a living reproach for the inadequacies of those who get stuck somewhere in their uphill climb.

All high-status male occupations have opened their doors to women, at least by a wide crack, over the past twenty years. The problem now begins at the other side of the door.

LIVING THE LAW

Law has become extraordinarily attractive for the new generation of women who live to work. From 6 percent in 1968 the numbers of women entering law school has skyrocketed to 31 percent of the total student body; in some law schools as many as 50 percent of the students are women.[10] Law offers status and potentially high income. These attractions are matched by long hours and high stress which the massive entry of women into the field has done little to change.

Admission to the bar does not require the crushing schedule of the internship/residency in medicine, but new lawyers are often expected to work sixty-plus hours each week during their first ten years or more. In many firms it is unheard of for an associate who has not yet made partner to leave the office before seven in the evening, and not to appear for at least part of the weekend. Law tends to be crisis oriented. It may be necessary to work around the clock before and during trial, or during an important negotiation.

In my own experience, law school itself was not impossibly demanding. It was a continuation of the kind of life I had led in college and in graduate school. I had a toddler when I entered law school, but I could easily arrange to pick him up at the baby-sitter's by five, to study at home when he was sick, and to go out for lunch with my friends on a regular basis. I also managed to teach at least one history course at a local university each semester.

My great awakening came when I began to practice law. Even though I had chosen what I thought would be a very low-key small firm where I would specialize in family law, the uncontrollable hours soon overwhelmed me. Leaving the office at a set hour to pick up my son at child care was a necessity, but not one that my clients or the courts could respect. Missing a court appearance because my child had strep throat was not looked upon with judicial tolerance. I was far from being a superwoman. Although I probably had sufficient ambition, energy, and intelligence, I did not have the money for reliable live-in help, nor did I have a husband to help out.

A woman lawyer who chose a job as an assistant U.S. attorney in which trials were an important part of her practice related this domestic juggling act:

> My husband and I were sort of balancing schedules on weekends. I would come in one day and he'd go into his office the other day, and when we started the trial I asked my regular baby sitter to come about 8:00 in the morning, then I'd have a teenager from the neighborhood come at 5:00 so our regular baby sitter could leave between 5:00 and 5:30 and then she'd stay till my husband could get home between 8:00 and 9:00. It was really a juggling act so my mother was coming for Thanksgiving vacation with my father, and we just asked her to stay on, and she stayed with us until a week before Christmas, when she took my son with her, and we brought him back after Christmas, and did the same thing with the regular baby sitter and the local baby sitter until the verdict.[11]

Law is rigidly hierarchical. There is an enormous gulf in terms of prestige, income, and the nature of the work between a partner in a large established law firm and a sole practitioner. Not only will the partner earn at least $200,000 each year while the sole practitioner may earn far less than $40,000, but the type of clients and the law practiced are entirely different. The partner may have corporate clients, who are rarely visible, and his or her work may be negotiating and overseeing various kinds of business deals. The sole practitioner may perform a wide range of services from divorces through personal injuries and wills, and usually has far more client contact than desired. In between the large-firm partner and the sole practitioner are judges, law professors, government attorneys, and in-house corporate counsels. Other kinds of lawyers fill a variety of private and public legal slots. Most lawyers rarely see the inside of a courtroom.

Within this hierarchy women traditionally clustered in certain "female" specialty areas such as trusts and estates, domestic relations, and tax law. If employed in a large firm they almost always remained associates, never achieving the status of partner. They were also represented in greater proportion than their numbers in government and in solo practice. All of these niches in the legal hierarchy allowed for a degree of control over time and usually involved little litigation, which is universally considered the most stressful aspect of law practice. These jobs often required a good deal of client contact, for which women were considered particularly well suited.

The explosion of huge numbers of women into the profession has done little to change this established pattern. In 1984, while women represented 30 percent of associates employed by a group of law firms surveyed by the National Law Journal, only 5 percent of the partnership positions were occupied by women. The

National Center for State Courts reports that only 4 percent of judges nationwide are women.[12]

Discrimination is only one of the factors which send women into female specialties. The avoidance which many young women lawyers exhibit toward the highly competitive jobs at the top is not strictly sinister cultural-conditioning, as many feminists would assert; it is a very real reluctance to take on a job that overwhelms all of one's public and most of one's private life. Most young women are unable to abandon at least the possibility of motherhood. The 1983 Supreme Court decision *Hishone v. King and Spaulding* confirmed that sex discrimination is forbidden in partnership decisions in law firms, just as it is in corporate promotions, but women must play the male-partnership game in order to win that slot.

The career clock of law is firmly set. Young recruits are hired immediately out of law school and are expected to follow a clearly timed path. Until recently it was rare to change law firms once you were in the harness. Dropping out for several years or even several months virtually guarantees that you are permanently out of the race. Pregnancy leaves or even reasonable vacations are rarely available, and part-time work has not been a part of the traditional law firm's structure; when they are offered, part-time jobs usually involve only the most routine or tedious legal tasks. Many women find that the only way they can have a family is to drop out of law entirely.

The way in which legal services are offered is changing radically. The economics of law practice dictate ever larger firms, with more and more branches. The sole practitioner is becoming almost as obsolete as last year's computer. Because of high overhead, particularly skyrocketing malpractice premiums, sole practitioners find it difficult to make a living, much more so a fortune. This is bad news for women, many of whom chose to become sole practitioners or worked as a husband/wife team while raising a family so that they could better control their time.

Women in law have already formed strong grass-roots organizations. Nearly every county bar now has a women lawyers' section, and there are several national organizations. Women lawyers are also very well represented in larger women's organizations like the National Women's Political Caucus and the National Organization for Women.

Women lawyers have become the generals and the soldiers for the equal-rights crusade, but they have made little or no attempt to change the working conditions of their own profession to make it bearable for women with children. They have strongly encouraged one another to go for the partner job or to try for the judgeship, but they have, for the most part, insisted that women play the game as men play it. It is women lawyers who have strongly opposed the maternity-leave statutes in California, Montana, and other states; and it is women lawyers who have held back on affirmative action, accepting the position that it gives special preference to women. The same women's bar meeting which provides child care so that its members can attend may well be discussing strategy on defeating the maternity-leave statute.

Women lawyers are in both a good and a bad position to secure a strong and viable place for themselves within the profession. They are in a bad position because the field is overcrowded, and in many urban areas there are not enough jobs to go around. Women often feel (rightly or wrongly) that if they ask for what they consider special privileges in terms of maternity leave, part-time work, regular hours, good vacation and sick leave, or full consideration at reentry, they will only get a boot out the door, to be replaced by an eager young man.

Women lawyers are in a good position to change their profession, because they are well organized on both a local and a national basis. Because of their numbers and their organization they could put pressure on employers in both the private and the public sectors to provide career paths that are compatible with family life. What is traditional is not necessarily efficient or economical. A career track which allows a woman to be an associate for many years with a reduced work load and the option of becoming a partner with full responsibilities when her children are grown could provide the stability and continuity of a good lawyer at a lower cost to the firm. In most specialty areas, outside of trial practice, there is no real reason why the lawyer must work a sixty-hour week. Organized women could bring pressure for affirmative action programs in which older reentry women could be considered equally with younger women for judgeships, corporate law, and other areas which are dominated by men.

In order to bring about this transformation in law practice, a reorientation of thinking by women lawyers must take place. Getting your foot in the door is useful only if there is something inside the door that brings more satisfaction than frustration. Equality with male lawyers is a self-destructive route. A legal career which offers special consideration for the lives of working mothers should be top priority.

Organized women lawyers are also in a strong position to help all women. The energy and resources that their organizations have devoted to the ERA could be channeled into the real need for family-law reform, publicly supported day care, guaranteed medical care for women and children, etc. They could use their political clout to insist that all candidates for office include women's issues in their platforms. Because of their organization, education, and political skills women lawyers could become the leaders of the reformulated women's-rights campaign.

MAKING IT IN MEDICINE

"It sounds sick to feel like a failure with all this education, but I do," confessed my friend Susan, who is just entering her last year of combined internship/residency in obstetrics and has already decided to take what she considers a "copout" job as a clinical supervisor of other residents when she finishes. Susan has endured a schedule that most human beings could not tolerate. Her daughter Amy, now three, was born during her last year of medical school. When Susan began her residency she had a full-time live-in baby-sitter and an obliging husband with a flexible university teaching schedule as support for her 110-hour work weeks. "Often I would come home after thirty-six hours or so and simply fall into bed until my next hitch. There were times when I didn't see my daughter for several days." The live-in baby-sitter turned out to have serious defects, and the house often looked as though it had been recently visited by a hurricane, but Susan could not fire her and take the risk of being without support. In this final year of her residency, her husband has accepted a better job at a distant university and will be only a weekend father. "I'm really not sure whether I'll be able to make it," she confided.

Susan has most of the characteristics of a super-woman—ambition, intelligence, a supportive husband, and enough money to hire household help—but even these are not enough to overcome the physical demands required by the double load of medical training and motherhood. She had originally planned to go into academic medicine, the high-status pinnacle of the profession, but she now feels unable to face the competition, stress and long hours required to make it to the top. Unfortunately, to her, compromise feels like failure.

The sleepless rigors of internships and residencies are legendary and often become the war stories of older physicians. There are many critics of the system, among them those who doubt that top medical care is delivered by sleep-deprived zombies, but women themselves have been reluctant to challenge the system. They fear that any criticism of the requirements would be viewed as asking for special favors and would jeopardize their careers. On an individual basis they have reason to fear. A third-year medical student described the reaction to her request to change the order of her clerkships.

> I'd taken all of my third year clerkships until the last two and I was really tired, really exhausted. I went to the Dean and I said, Look, I don't want to take ob/gyn this month. I'm planning on going into that field and I'm too tired to do it justice. I'd just as soon take radiology. I've never been so hassled in my entire medical career. He threatened me with the fact that I would be ruining my career, that they would think I was too weak.[13]

The number of women entering medical school has climbed spectacularly in recent years, from 13.7 percent in 1971 to 33.9 percent or more in the eighties,[14] but their numbers have made little impact on the structure of the profession. So far the medical profession has funneled most of them into the areas traditionally served by women doctors: clinic jobs, HMO (health maintenance organization) facilities, pediatrics, student health, etc. The high-status, high-paying specialties in academic medicine, surgery, or orthopedics have remained male territory.

The reasons for extreme sex segregation within medicine are complex. Certainly some men have actively worked to keep women out of prestige specialties, but usually the career choice is more subtle. The high-status specialties are perceived as high-stress also, with uncontrollable hours. Today's women medical students, unlike the spinster "hen medics" of previous eras, want, at least abstractly, to have a family as well as a career. In order to survive the split commitment, they will choose the areas where they have more control of their time and where they experience less stress.

Medicine, like most prestigious professions, forces its participants into a career clock based on a male model. In order to reach the top, a surgeon or an academic in medicine is expected to reach a certain level of achievement at age thirty-five, forty-five, etc. A man who drops out of the race for ten years is not allowed to reenter and achieve at forty-five what he was expected to achieve at thirty-five. One can speed up the career clock, but one cannot slow it down.

Unfortunately the peak productivity years in the male model fall during the peak child-rearing years of a woman's life. If women could take on lessened responsibility for ten years or so during their child-rearing years, they might well be able to reenter the race with more maturity and better organizational skills. The current model does not allow this.

The kinds of medical jobs that are suitable for women with families often suffer from the same problems of relatively low pay (compared with the profession as a whole) and lack of imagination that are common to all female-dominated occupations. My own woman doc-

tor, a board-certified internist, told me of her first job
at Kaiser Permanente Medical Center in Oakland, California, the grandfather of the HMO movement. With
two young children, she chose to work part time. At
that time, in the mid-seventies, Kaiser accepted part-
time workers, but only in its drop-in nonemergency
clinic, not in specialty areas. "I tried to argue with the
head of the Internal Medicine Department that the
Bay Area was the national center for the women's
movement and it would be good politics to have a
woman on the staff, but he wouldn't budge." In her
opinion there was no rational basis for disallowing part-
time specialists, since Kaiser doctors were not available
at any time for individual patients, but operated on a
rotating basis. She has since found a happier niche with
a small group practice. If one of her children is sick, the
child can lie on a couch in an empty examination room
to be checked between appointments, and she is on call
only one night a week. "I still go into deep depressions
before school holidays," she commented, echoing the
feeling of all working mothers. "I never know what to
do with them when school is out and I have to work."[15]

Like almost all women who live to work, women doctors have defined the problem as personal, rather than
structural, and the solution as solely their responsibility. One woman doctor with three children described
her attempt to bend the system rather than take all the
responsibility on her back: "When I was a resident I
went so far overboard, I had to be the perfect resident.
With this last child, I had the confidence to ask the system to bend for me. I would bring the baby-sitter to
work sometimes, and sometimes my husband came over.
Women deprive themselves of a lot. I find it's so important not to drop out altogether."[16]

Very few women would have the confidence to act in

such an unorthodox manner on an individual basis, and in fact the response to such behavior may not be as warm as this woman's experience. The only way in which women can bend the system to be more suitable to women with families is through organized group efforts—through the professional organizations like the American Medical Association and its local affiliates. With their growing numbers, women are in a strong position to take this on.

There is no easy solution to the problem that both medicine and motherhood are enormously demanding of both time and commitment; but it is also true, as is shown by the example of the HMOs, that medicine does not have to be a twenty-hour-a-day commitment. Women can certainly work on the thorny problems of internship/residency, part-time employment in specialty areas, and a different career track that allows reentry on a full-time serious basis in midlife. An affirmative-action program that gives special preference to older returning women in high-status academic and specialty areas could be a goal as well.

In some ways, women in medicine are already more fortunate than women who live to work in other professions. In most areas of the country doctors are in demand, and it is possible for women doctors to find a work schedule, either part time or full time, which allows them to stay in the profession, albeit under less than optimal conditions, during their intense child-rearing years. The growth of the HMO movement as a response to the economic crisis in medicine may provide an unexpected windfall for women. The HMO structure provides a controlled work week which has become very attractive to many men as well as women. If the HMO model becomes the norm, women will find the battle of integration into all areas of medicine far easier to win.

CAREER VERSUS FAMILY

The conflict between a demanding career and marriage and children is not new; what is new is that women are attempting to accomplish both, rather than choosing between them.

By 1890 women were at least represented in virtually all the male-dominated professions. Women with great courage and tough skins had demanded and won places in medicine, law, journalism and higher education. By 1910 the percentage of women in many male-dominated professions reached a level that continued to recent times. For instance, the percentage of women doctors at the turn of the century was 7 percent, and it was 7 percent in 1970 as well.[17]

But unlike modern women, educated women in the nineteenth and early twentieth centuries did not agonize over career versus marriage or over marriage in addition to a career. It was accepted as an either/or decision. Either a woman married and became a mother or she remained single and followed a career. Only 50 percent of those graduating from women's colleges married in 1890, while most of the unmarried pursued a career.[18] In general the overwhelming majority of women in the nineteenth century who worked outside the home were single; only 4 percent of all married women worked.[19]

Women who lived to work in the nineteenth and early twentieth centuries had a qualitatively different experience from that of modern women. Very few were wives or mothers, and therefore they did not face the overwhelming difficulties of balancing motherhood and career. But they lived in a culture that firmly held that motherhood, not career, was the highest calling for women. They had to deal with the not-very-subtle attitudes of both men and women that they followed a career because they could not get a husband. Whether or not they were active suffragists, they were viewed with the same suspicion that spinster Susan B. Anthony suffered as an early feminist. In the nineteenth century spinster suffragists and career women alike were caricatured as ugly, shrewish, and strong-minded.[20]

By the 1920s a trend had begun for more women to marry after college, and for at least some of those women to combine careers and marriage. Women's colleges attempted to take up the challenge practically. Experiments were begun with cooperative nurseries, communal laundries, and the age-old panacea, central kitchens. The ideas of radical feminist Charlotte Perkins Gilman, who advocated large apartment complexes with general kitchens, cleaning services, and nurseries staffed by professionals to relieve mothers' burdens, were enthusiastically discussed.[21]

The Depression aborted this budding trend of career and marriage. It was considered immoral for women at all levels to take over men's work. The patriotic call of World War II brought many married women into the work force, but the war machine needed welders more than it needed lawyers. It was not until the war was won and peacetime prosperity produced many new jobs in the service and professional sectors that married women with high ambitions were tempted back into the career field.

The women's movement has had an important influence on women who live to work. When my generation of women who were in high school or college in the sixties read about "the problem that has no name" in Betty Friedan's *The Feminine Mystique*, we could only vaguely imagine what it would be like to be a frustrated housewife with too much education and too few intellectual outlets. We resolved that we would not become prisoners in our own home. We would instead go out into the world and seek the power and glory that had been reserved to men and let the home take care of itself. We were unaware that the conflict between career and family had been encountered earlier by American women, because for the most part we were quite unhistorical. When we did learn about women's history it was too often presented as an evolutionary pageant in which women gradually broke the chains that tied them to the patriarchal bedpost, to arrive at the current point in history where they could compete for the prizes that had been selfishly hogged by men.

MAKING IT WORK

Modern women who live to work have faced the century-old conflict between career and family by pretending it doesn't exist. Title VII and the Equal Rights Amendment are bold statements that there is no problem—women can do things on the same terms on which men have always done them. But women who live to work need more than Title VII or the ERA with their punitive egalitarian logic. They need, as do all working women, the special consideration of pregnancy or parental leaves; they need the extra boost of affirmative action to initiate them into male bailiwicks; they need the guaranteed support of child care. They need these special considerations because they bear the special burden of child-rearing.

And women who live to work need additional consideration. Because they have chosen highly competitive male professions, they have taken on highly competitive time and stress demands as well. In order to find permanent integration within these professions, women must carve career paths which allow for the reality of motherhood. This means shattering the male career clock to make way for a child-raising hiatus of lessened job responsibility followed by active reentry. It means lobbying for meaningful part-time work at fair wages. It means convincing employers that it is in their economic best interest to hire stable professionals on a reduced-hour, reduced-income basis, with the possibility of expanded responsibility down the road.

Women already have the organizations within their professions that could take on this mandate. Women lawyers, women doctors, and women academics are relatively well organized, as are women in most other highly competitive professions. It is a matter of rethinking priorities and not being afraid to challenge the male model.

For instance, women lawyers (or men if they chose) could initiate an optional partnership track where they could work twenty or thirty hours a week for a period up to ten years of child-raising before being considered for partner. (The baby track?) In professions which demand exceptionally long hours, part-time work may be as much as forty hours a week, on a regular schedule. Or women could initiate a permanent part-time track where they would gain a permanent position, perhaps an associate partnership, after a number of years, but not full partnership rights. This model could be adapted for the university world and the medical professions as well.

Small cracks are occurring in the rigid male career track, but as yet they are too few and too often based on individual exceptions rather than general policy. In California, the State Bar's Committee on Women in the Law has at last taken up the issue of part-time employment for women with children. In a survey of sixty-eight Los Angeles firms with more than twenty attorneys the good news is that eleven firms have women working half to three-quarter time. All of these women have small children; none is on the partnership track. These women are all compensated either according to the percentage of time worked or as a percentage of hours billed. Two firms even have part-time women partners. The bad news is that the other fifty-seven firms have no part-time women attorneys and the eleven that do made the accommodation on an individual basis. The criterion was that the woman had previously been a valued full-time employee or was considered to be someone very special.[22]

Managerial positions that require supervising other full-time employees create obvious practical problems. What will the employees do if the boss is not there to watch them? Not all employees need supervision every minute, but in those instances where this is necessary a job-sharing arrangement may be possible.

There are very few high-status jobs that could not be cut down or cut up to fit mothers if organized effort and imagination were put into it, but there probably are some. Mothers may have to temporarily abandon jobs that involve a great deal of travel, such as international correspondent or airline pilot, and retreat to the desk for a few years. But the right of reentry should be strongly asserted.

Affirmative action should also be an important strategy for women who live to work. In order to create career paths that allow for greater control of time and stress and allow for periods of withdrawal and reentry, women must be well represented in all areas of their chosen professions and they must act forcefully in their own interests. Affirmative action in male professions should include not only special preference for entry-level jobs, but special preference for middle-aged reentry women. As long as the percentage of women who are orthopedic surgeons or labor lawyers or university professors is small, the specialty does not need to bend to their needs.

But in fact women who live to work have long ago given up on affirmative action, if indeed they ever embraced it, and have left it largely as a strategy for racial minorities. Affirmative action was introduced as a concept which would work hand in glove with Title VII of the Civil Rights Act of 1964. The theory was that Title VII not only covers current discrimination in employment against race, creed, national origin, and (as a last-minute addition) sex, but could also be applied to make up for past offenses as well. Employers must set goals or quotas which would allow racial minorities and women to "catch up."

The contradictions in the theory of affirmative action soon became apparent. Given the slippery nature of egalitarian thinking, righting past inequalities inevitably creates current inequalities. If women and racial minorities are given special preference in hiring, white men will suffer discrimination. In fact, criticism of affirmative action claimed that Title VII itself must be interpreted to forbid special preference to any group, thus prohibiting affirmative action.

The issue of reverse discrimination came to the attention of the Supreme Court in a series of cases, the first of which, Bakke v. Board of Regents (1978), dealt not with employment but with special admissions. Bakke, a white male student, contended that he was denied admission to medical school because several places were reserved for racial minorities. He contended that he was better qualified than the minority students who filled these slots, and that he was not receiving equal protection under the law as guaranteed by the Fourteenth Amendment to the Constitution.

Faced with a constitutional Gordian knot, the Supreme Court hedged and basically said that special preference to right past inequalities was not in itself unconstitutional, but quota systems which reserved specific slots for minorities for which other applicants could not compete violated the Fourteenth Amendment.[23]

Over the next nine years the Court seesawed and puzzled over the inherent contradictions of affirmative action, giving the Reagan Administration the courage to attempt to dismantle voluntary public affirmative-action programs. Organized women did not fight back. Affirmative action was dropped from the top-priority lists of the major feminist organizations, NOW and NWPC, leaving the defense to the civil rights groups such as the National Association for the Advancement of Colored People.[24]

Ironically, it was in a case involving a woman, not a member of a racial minority, that the Supreme Court decided to make a firm stand supporting affirmative action in 1987. The case began in 1980 when Diane Joyce was promoted over Paul Johnson to a job dispatching road crews in Santa Clara County, California, even though he had scored slightly higher in the interviews. For the first time, the Court held that an employer did not have to show proof of past discrimination against women or minorities in order to use sexual and racial preferences in hiring and promotions to bring its work force in line with the makeup of the local population. Justice Brennan, delivering the majority opinion, stated, "Given the obvious imbalance in the skilled craft category in favor of men and against women, it was plainly not unreasonable . . . to consider the sex of Ms. Joyce in making its decision."[25]

Generally organized feminist groups greeted this decision with approval, but some women agreed with Linda Chavez, former staff director of the United States Commission on Civil Rights, who commented, "In my view, the women's movement was aimed at allowing women to compete on an equal footing without regard to sex, and I think what this decision does is return us to the nineteenth-century concept that says women are the weaker sex and need special protections in order to be able to compete."[26]

With this affirmative-action decision, and with the previously discussed 1986 decision which permitted statutory maternity leaves (*California Federal Savings and Loan Association v. Guerra*), the Supreme Court has sprung the equality trap for women. It has taken the position that preferential rather than equal treatment is the solution to some of the problems that face working women.

Now it is up to women to take the lead set by the Court and press for affirmative action on all fronts. Affirmative-action plans in the private sector are voluntary on the part of the employers. No employer will initiate a controversial affirmative-action plan unless strongly pressed to do so. Women who live to work must put pressure on their employers, both individually and through their professional organizations, to create or reinstitute affirmative-action plans which have been dropped. They must also expand the scope of these plans to give additional preference to older women who are reentering the field. Affirmative action must acknowledge the pattern of women's work lives.

7

WOMEN
WHO WORK TO LIVE

Women who work to live toil in a wide variety of jobs ranging from domestic worker and factory operative to teacher and nurse. Their common ground is that they work in female-dominated occupations and are generally poorly paid. Their attitudes toward their work vary with the status of the work they perform, but most of these women work because they need the money. Unlike their sisters who are plunging into high-status male-dominated professions, these women do not find their primary gratification and identification in their work; for many it is something they must endure in order to survive.

Women who work to live also share the "myth of the temporary worker." For the most part they believe that they will be rescued from working. In this myth the rescue may take place when they find a husband to support them, when a child is born, when the down payment for the house is saved, etc. The reality is that there will be no rescue. With the demise of the family wage these women are destined to be lifelong, not temporary, workers. The myth has become self-destructive to women who are not willing to put in the time and energy to improve what they consider to be a temporary job.

These are the women, not their sisters with attaché cases, who make up most of the vast growing bulge of women entering or reentering the job market. They are the workers who operate the word processors and process the food in our fast-expanding information/service economy. The apparent prosperity of the country has depended upon drawing ever more of these women into jobs where there are few unions or organizations to bargain for higher wages or health benefits. The 13 percent drop in the wages of the average worker between 1973 and 1985[1] reflects the new low wage structure. Many women who work to live can work full time year round and still not rise above the poverty level.

Women who work to live are not the darlings of the egalitarian revolution, which looks up toward the male-dominated professions, not down toward the female-dominated occupations. The competitive model of Title VII has had little impact on these workers, since for the most part they work in enclaves of other female workers where there are few men with whom to compete.

Only with comparable worth, the recently embraced strategy for helping working women, have feminists begun to break free of the equality trap and look to the problems of at least some women who work in female enclaves. Comparable worth recognizes that most women are not able to improve their lot by leaving their jobs to compete with men. The female-dominated occupations often offer them control of their time and energy which is necessary for women with families. Comparable worth argues that the pay scale of female-dominated occupations should be compared and adjusted upward to conform to male-dominated occupations with similar education, responsibility, and skill.

But the problems of women who work to live are far too varied to be treated by a single solution. Women nurses and women factory workers share the experience of working in female occupations, but these occupations have different traditions, demand different skills, and require different paths to improvement. In order to understand these variations, in this chapter I will divide women who work to live into manual workers, clerical workers, and workers in female professions.

MANUAL WORKERS

I always dream I'm alone and things are quiet. I call it the land of no-phone, where there isn't any machine telling me where I have to be every minute. The machine dictates, this crummy little machine with buttons on it—you've got to be there to answer it. You can walk away from it and pretend you don't hear it, but it pulls you. You know you're not doing anything, not doing a hell of a lot for anyone. Your job doesn't mean anything. Because *you're* just a little machine. A monkey could do what I do. It's really unfair to ask someone to do that.[2]

Sharon, telephone receptionist, is one of the swelling army of women who work to live. Sharon and other women manual workers. They work because they must, they work for the paycheck. If given the option they would probably not work at all, certainly not at the jobs they now hold.

Manual workers hold very different attitudes toward work from women who live to work. Manual laborers don't see work as challenging or glamorous, with business lunches in good restaurants and a "dress for success" wardrobe. They see work as demeaning, exhausting, and mind-wearying. Work is hard on the body and deadening to the soul.

It is not only the women who feel negatively about jobs in which they become an appendage of a machine, or where their bodies are the machine itself. As Studs Terkel found when interviewing workers in all occupations for his book *Working*, men find manual labor as stupefying as women do.[3]

There are, however, at least two important differences between men and women manual laborers. When a man gets off, he goes to a bar to let off steam and then home to watch television. He claims he is too tired to do anything else. When a woman factory worker gets off her shift, more likely in a textile rather than a steel factory, she faces hours of domestic and child-related chores. A male factory worker may go to a sports event on the weekend. A woman worker catches up on housework. But the most important difference between men and women manual laborers is that men will bring home bigger checks, about a dollar for every sixty cents carried home by women workers.

Because of their low wages, these are the women most likely to slip below the poverty line when they become the head of household as a result of divorce, death, or desertion. Full-time work at minimum wage will not lift a mother with children above this arbitrary line, and many of these women work in the unregulated fringe of the labor market as domestics or waitresses at below minimum wage. Even the mother who has spent all of her life in the comfortable middle class may find upon divorce that her skills give her entry only into the world of manual labor.

About thirteen million women work for industries or businesses in jobs that need their bodies more than their brains and require little or no formal training or education. These women are machine operators, particularly in apparel manufacturing and in textile and knitting mills; operators in laundries and dry-cleaning establishments; dressmakers outside of factories; assemblers in certain manufacturing industries such as electrical-component manufacturing; packers and wrappers in all kinds of establishments; operators in telephone and other communications industries; beauticians, waitresses, hospital aides and orderlies, chambermaids; and, of course, household domestics.

Women manual workers usually come from working-class or poor families. They often have less than a high-school education. They marry working-class men and work because of financial need. Frequently they are the sole breadwinner. Manual workers represent about 40 percent of all employed women, and about 60 percent of black women workers. Black women work harder and get paid less than everyone else, including white women. Both black and white women laborers are segregated from their male counterparts. Men manual workers are craftsmen in construction and other industries; they are foremen, mechanics, repairmen, printers, transportation equipment operators, bus, taxi, and truck drivers, police and firemen and guards. Even when they hold the same job description as women, such as factory operative, they work in different industries—e.g., men labor in steel mills and women labor in textile mills.[4]

Since the nineteenth century, women have held most of the manual-labor jobs they hold today, but they held them only until they married. It was an accepted part of the working-class culture, as well as the middle-class culture, that a man supported his family. A wife who worked outside the home would bring public shame to the husband. In the two decades following World War II this cultural perception gradually shifted. Inflation and a shift away from heavy manufacturing broke the family wage structure, making it impossible for a blue-collar husband to support his family as his father had done. At the same time the huge growth in the service sector expanded many manual-labor jobs that had always been considered women's jobs, like telephone operators and chambermaids. Today the pressure is on women to return to their jobs as soon as possible after the children are born, to regard childbirth like a serious flu which can be treated by a month or so of sick leave.

Manual laborers have been systematically ignored by the women's movement with its focus on the top of women's occupations, not the bottom. This is a sharp break from feminists of the nineteenth and early twentieth centuries who put a great deal of their energy and concern into improving the lot of women manual workers. Women manual workers are the fastest growing but least visible part of the huge phenomenon of women entering the labor market. Legislation and legal actions aimed at achieving equality in the workplace have passed them by. Since they work for the most part with enclaves of other women, there are no men with whom to compete. The competitive model of Title VII has had almost no impact on these workers, nor has the concept of equal pay for equal work. In fact, there are indications that this group of women is losing rather than gaining ground compared with men manual workers (usually in different industries).[5] Historically, the way in which manual workers have greatly improved their lot is through unions. When I was growing up in the iron-ore range of northern Minnesota, John L. Lewis and Franklin Delano Roosevelt were considered household saints for their contributions to unionization. Before the United Mine Workers and the National Labor Relations Board the life of the miner had too often been nasty, brutish, and cut short by an industrial accident. My grandfather told me how he worked twelve to sixteen hours each day in dirty, hazardous conditions to earn a wage that barely supported the family, only to be cut off from work entirely in slack seasons. My grandmother took in boarders all her life to hold the family together.

There is no question that unionization improves wages for both men and women no matter what their occupation. But, unfortunately, unions have helped the working man more than they have helped the working woman. Three out of ten male workers in the United States are union members, compared with only one out of seven women workers. Male-dominated unions have often discriminated against women workers, but, more important, there are vast numbers of women working in areas that have been untouched by unions.[6]

The relationship between women and unions has been a troubled one. The earliest trade unions, in the early nineteenth century, were entirely male, but as early as 1830 women workers showed an interest in joining male trade unions or forming their own. As a rule, if women were in a trade at the time it was unionized they were accepted into the union. If they were not, the unions were used to keep them out. Union leaders firmly believed that women would always work for less and therefore would bring down the wage structure. They also believed that women considered themselves temporary workers who would be rescued by marriage. For the most part this was true. The percentage of married women who continued working outside the home was very low until the recent phenomenon of married women flooding the labor market. As a result, the numbers of women in unions has been consistently low. In 1910, for instance, it is estimated that the total number of women workers organized by all unions was no more than 75,000 out of more than eight million women in the labor force.[7]

Women themselves have been reluctant to organize. Young unmarried women until recently have made up the bulk of the labor force, and they have looked upon their work as a temporary activity until marriage. Women have also been sensitive to the criticism and sexual slurs (including frequent comparison to prostitutes) that were used to describe women who participated in labor unions or who went on strike.[8] Some women, like Mother Jones, who spent her life organizing coal miners and mill workers, were fiery activists, but the majority were not.

Because they received no special protection from unions, working women looked to the middle-class women's-rights reformers for help, and they got it. The majority of feminists in the first part of the twentieth century strongly supported protective legislation for women. In fact, one of the chief arguments for suffrage was that women would use the vote to promote more protective legislation. It was considered a major victory for women when most states passed laws which put such limitations on work as the kinds of tasks, hours, and conditions of work, and a minimum wage for women.[9] Some of the negative aspects of such legislation were soon apparent: it allowed unions and employers to restrict women from certain occupations by raising the hourly requirements above the legislative level. But it was widely believed that this legislation improved the lot of the factory laborer. Only two groups took exception to the almost uniform belief that protective legislation helped women workers: the National Association of Manufacturers, which found such legislation costly, and the supporters of Alice Paul's National Women's Party, who carried the banner of the ERA.[10]

It may be that the kind of protective legislation for women that the early feminists fought for is no longer necessary, since most states now have health and safety regulations, minimum-wage laws and hourly regulations that apply to men as well as women. But a different kind of protective legislation is critically needed now that women with children are in the work force. Pregnancy leaves which guarantee a return to the same job (this is what NOW and NWPC actively opposed in California Federal Savings and Loan Association v. Guerra) and which guarantee child care are special needs of all working women, but are critical for manual laborers who cannot afford private child care or the loss of a job due to childbirth. Protection against forced overtime or swing shifts for working mothers is just as critical as the eight-hour day was for their unmarried ancestors. A higher minimum wage, which would apply to men as well as women, would be a great boost for nonunionized women in the lowest-paying jobs. Sixty-five percent of all minimum-wage workers are women.

What women who perform manual labor want more than protective legislation, more meaningful work, or even child care, is a better wage. In the scant literature on low-income working women, the need to put food on the table and pay the bills is paramount. The road to higher wages is long and rocky, and it requires more than one strategy. In general, women can organize to improve the wages in the jobs they already hold, or they can attempt to take the higher-paid blue-collar jobs now held by men.

Lack of skilled training is the major reason that most women manual workers are stuck where they are in female-dominated pools. Cultural attitudes shared by the women themselves discourage them from obtaining skilled training at school or on the job in apprenticeships. The same attitude of impermanence that discourages women from putting effort into organizing also keeps them away from the vocational training and apprenticeships that are necessary to make Rosie a riveter. This attitude is reinforced by schools and unions, who are the gatekeepers to the higher-paying skilled jobs. They also perceive women as temporary workers and therefore not suitable for training. In many school systems serious vocational training is not even available to women, despite continued increases in funds for vocational training and laws against sex discrimination in education. In 1972 over half the students in vocational courses were women, but only 55 percent of the women students were enrolled in courses preparing them for earning a living; the others were in homemaking programs. The majority of those in job-oriented courses were in a secretarial/business track. Only 9 percent were enrolled in technical programs, such as electrical, mechanical, plumbing, drafting, or dental or medical assistance.[11]

The Title VII strategy championed by middle-class feminists is of little use to women in female-dominated occupations which require little or no skill. Most often the barriers to their competing with men are those of skill rather than sex discrimination. Only by increasing their skills can they crack the barriers of the male-dominated trades.

Working-class women themselves must take the initiative to obtain skilled training and to transform cultural attitudes. They must acknowledge their new reality as lifelong rather than temporary workers and insist that they and their daughters receive skilled and technical training to enter the male trades. Since many of the traditional male trades are losing ground in the shift away from manufacturing, women must be trained in the new trades, such as computer programming, and electronics manufacturing and repair as well.

But entering male-dominated skill trades has many of the same problems for working-class women that entering male professions has for middle-class women. While a woman doctor or lawyer may be overwhelmed by the time commitments the profession demands and may not be able to balance family and work commitments, a woman manual laborer may find that after driving a big rig or riveting, even for eight hours, she is too exhausted physically to return home to make dinner for the family and complete the household chores that no one else is going to take on. It is far easier to stay on the mindless, low-stress routine of an assembly line.

There has been a continuing flap in Title VII circles over the BFOQ (bonafide occupational qualification). Feminists claim that employers advertise many jobs with false height and weight qualifications in order to keep women out and to gain an exemption from Title VII. This is undoubtedly true, but the other side of the coin is true also: there are many hard physical-labor jobs that women, no matter what their strength, cannot combine with the demands of motherhood. Encouraging women who have children (or who will eventually have children) to take them on will only set them up for failure, as it does women doctors and lawyers who take on men's schedules. The argument, used by Louis D. Brandeis in 1923 to promote the eight-hour day, that women workers must be protected because they will be future mothers is a practical truth. Women may not be weaker than men physically, but they must bear the everyday burdens of parenthood in a way men do not.

Does this mean women should not strive to become, say, skilled industrial workers? Women should certainly be encouraged to demand skilled training, but they should also be given a realistic idea of the physical demands of each of the trades before they start something they cannot continue as mothers. Job counseling should be introduced with the beginning of vocational training. As with all male-dominated occupations, including those in the professions, getting in the door is only the beginning of the battle; balancing the job with family obligations is the real fight. Some skills, such as electrical wiring, are surely less demanding physically than carpet-laying or welding. Another route is to demand, through union collective bargaining, part-time work or reduced shifts. Initially this seems radical, but employers have learned to come down from the twelve-hour day to the ten-hour day and now to the eight-hour day. There are undoubtedly many men who would welcome this option as well.

Following skilled training, affirmative action, first at the apprentice level and then at the hiring level, would provide a good boost to women striving to enter the male-dominated skilled trades. Thus far, affirmative action has been only weakly applied as a national policy and, because of its nonegalitarian nature, has not been politically embraced by the women's movement. The recent Supreme Court decision upholding a voluntary affirmative-action policy in *Johnson v. Transportation Agency* may push this important strategy forward. Union women, through such organizations as the Coalition of Labor Union Women, are in a strong position

to demand preferential hiring for women in collective-
bargaining agreements.

A major push to enforce the largely ignored Executive Order 11246, issued in 1965 by Lyndon Johnson,
which requires all federal contractors to set goals and
timetables for eliminating imbalances in hiring, and to
make "good faith" efforts to meet these goals, could
potentially affect about 100,000 companies and institutions. This could be used as one tool among many to
pull women workers out of their low-paying ruts.

The combination of unions and increased skills offers
the best strategy for women manual laborers to push
their way into the male-dominated skilled trades, and
unions also offer the best prospect of improving the
conditions of the jobs women already hold in female
occupations. Realistically, even with the best possible
training opportunities, there will always be women
(and men as well) who will remain in unskilled manual-labor jobs. It is just as important to raise their pay
and conditions as it is to promote women to higher-
skilled jobs through training.

Unfortunately, all the same old problems that have
persisted during the past 150 years confront organizers
who attempt to organize women today, and some new
ones have been added. The rate of union membership
for both men and women has fallen in the past decade.
The general decline in manufacturing has been reflected by a decline in union membership. The unions
have suffered in prestige because of a few well-known
incidents in which union leaders, like Jimmy Hoffa of
the Teamsters, used their tremendous power to promote
their private interests. Japanese competition and the
Japanese model of corporate solidarity, rather than
workers' unions, have been particularly devastating for
some industrial unions, most notably the United Auto
Workers.

But unions, traditionally unfriendly, if not hostile, to women workers, have come a long way toward recognizing the needs of women workers. This change has come about through the activism of individual women union members, most notably through the Coalition of Labor Union Women, founded in 1973 to "bring together women trade union members to deal with our special concerns as unionists and women."[12] The CLUW was so successful in rousing consciousness that the AFL-CIO convention not only endorsed the ERA, which the organization had long opposed as a piece of threatening protective legislation, but, more important, put forward the most feminist platform in its history. In a pragmatic mixture of egalitarian and protectionist proposals, the AFL-CIO pledged to fight discrimination at the bargaining table and to press for child-care legislation and maternity-leave protection. Delegates endorsed full participation of women in all union activities and resolved to cooperate with the CLUW. George Meany described himself as a "closet feminist" and spoke at a national ERA rally while at the same time he encouraged Congress to require employers to provide regular disability benefits for pregnancy.[13]

Union leaders are awakening to the fact that they need women in order to survive. The AFL-CIO lost 2.7 million workers between 1980 and 1984, while the economy offered new jobs to 3.8 million workers. Most of these new jobs went to women, and most were in the vast, unorganized service sector.[14]

Unfortunately, women have not yet recognized that they need unions. The attitudes of working-class women themselves are still the greatest enemy of organization. In spite of the cold statistical realities of modern life, where the hard facts of inflation and divorce dictate that women will work throughout their adult life with very few breaks, most women manual laborers still consider their work as temporary and therefore not worth the bother of trying to change. As researcher Pamela Roby reports:

> West coast organizers for the United Electrical Workers express heartache from hearing dozens of women electrical workers in their twenties echo their employers, saying assuredly, I won't be working long— only until we pay for the washer and dryer (the car, our vacation, etc.)—I don't need to worry about how this job's treating me. The organizers know many women workers in their forties and fifties who held the same belief 10 years ago.[15]

Effective organization will come only when working women themselves want it. They must recognize themselves as permanent workers with sustained interest in skilled training, higher wages and better working conditions. They must impress this reality on their daughters and the vocational-training schools.

The women's movement could and should look down, not just up, and join with working women to help convince women manual laborers to organize as their feminist predecessors did with the Women's Trade Union League. But unions have been particularly unpopular with this generation of middle-class feminists because they have been unwilling to fight the Title VII cause. The competitive logic of Title VII is in direct conflict with the protective goal of unions. This was clearly shown when the Communications Workers of America fought the Title VII case brought by the Equal Employment Opportunities Commission against AT&T. The EEOC won a $15 million damage claim for women and minorities for "pervasive and systematic discrimination." The CWA argued that the agreement infringed upon collective-bargaining rights,[16] which of course it did. Unions are by their very nature nonegali-

tarian and opposed to free competition. The purpose of
a union is to protect a chosen group, the union members, from the arbitrary swings and exploitative wages
of a free market and to discriminate against nonunion
members in order to maintain improved conditions for
union workers.

There are hopeful signs that feminists have begun to
abandon the competitive logic of equal rights by em-
bracing comparable worth, or pay equity, as a solution
for the low pay of working women compared with men
in comparable jobs. With this theory, feminists acknowledge for the first time that most women are not
going to improve their position by leaving their female
occupations to compete with men in male occupations.
It is necessary to boost the female occupations, rather
than abandon them entirely for male jobs. The logic of
comparable worth is that the pay scale of female-
dominated occupations should be compared and adjusted upward to conform to male-dominated occupations which require similar education, responsibility,
and skill.

So far this new bargaining tool has been effectively
used mainly by public-employee unions focusing on
clerical work, not manual labor. Following the 1983
federal court decision *AFSCME v. Washington* (sub-
sequently overturned), in which the state of Washington was ordered to pay its women workers (mostly
clerical) $800 million in back pay, scores of municipal
and state employee unions are seeking to readjust their
pay scales. Although the private sector will offer strong
resistance, the combination of union organization and
comparable-worth strategy could aid women factory
operatives in textile mills to gain a salary comparable
to men factory operatives in steel mills.

There are other avenues of support for women manual laborers as well. Middle-class women who are not

otherwise politically active can give effective support by asserting consumer control through the old-fashioned but effective strategy of the boycott against companies that block the unionization of mainly women workers. In the early seventies there were many housewives who faithfully boycotted grapes to aid the organization of migrant workers. Similar effective boycotts were carried on against the linens produced by J. P. Stevens and the pants manufactured by Farah, companies that blocked union efforts.

CLERICAL WORKERS

"Word processing stinks," complained Susan, a word processor in a large law firm. "Every night I go home with a headache and a sore back. I can't even watch television after sitting in front of that damn screen all day. They told me I needed word-processing skills to make it in today's job market, but I didn't know it would hurt like this."

Susan commutes by public transportation from a suburban apartment to San Francisco. Each day she drives her three-year-old daughter to day care at seven-thirty, leaves her car at the subway station for a forty-five minute subway ride, and returns to pick up her daughter at six. "It's a long day, but I can't afford to live in the city, and jobs out here don't exist." Susan is a single parent who receives no support from her ex-husband and could not live on her salary if it were not for a small inheritance she received from her grandfather. About one in seven women clerical workers who head households has an income at or below the poverty level.

Susan is part of the great clerical army which is the fastest-growing area of employment in the United

States; the foot soldiers are almost all women. The great postwar transition away from manufacturing and toward service has produced an almost insatiable appetite for clerical workers to produce, control, and dispatch the paper that is the product of a service economy.

Clerical workers are different from their sisters who perform manual labor in factories or restaurants or homes. Their jobs require some manual skills (usually typing or word processing) and usually good communication skills as well. Many women clerical workers are educated far beyond the needs of their jobs. College diplomas are not an unusual credential for secretaries to hold, although they are rarely a job requirement. College-educated women often find they have no better offers.

Some women choose office work by taking specialized training in high school or a business college, but many choose it by default. This is in part because a liberal-arts college major does not attract flocks of employers, but it is also true that office work, because it is a woman's field and has been so for the past twenty years, is more accommodating to the needs of women than many of the occupations held by men with the same educational background. For the most part secretaries work nine to five with no overtime, and with not much responsibility to carry home. Evenings and weekends are free for family. Alternative fields chosen by men such as insurance salesman or junior account executive may pay more, but they demand more in terms of time and stress. Perhaps more important, office workers are not on a career clock. They can leave jobs and pick up jobs with relative ease after absences of months or even years devoted to child care. This is not so for the insurance salesman or the account executive, who must follow a clear career path without lengthy dropouts.

But automation has changed the nature of clerical work, and not usually for the better. Where Susan works, every lawyer used to have his or her own secretary. This was not necessarily more efficient, but it was surely more personal. On some days some secretaries would have very light loads. Secretaries and their bosses developed a team spirit, and some sort of human bond. In this age of automation there is one secretary for every two lawyers, and the "production typing" is given to the word processor. Susan and her machine share the same name and are treated as one—not quite human, not quite machine. In the office hierarchy, the word processor is rated below the legal secretary, despite similar pay, since she does not have the status of being attached to one or more attorneys. Susan does not have any close friends among the legal secretaries and paralegals in the office where she works, and she rarely talks to an attorney. "Last Christmas the office manager gave me a bottle of whiskey for my husband. I guess he didn't know I don't have a husband," she commented with a slight smile.

Office workers have been traditionally among the most difficult workers to organize, even though they are usually the most poorly paid of the skilled workers. As with manual workers, most secretaries and clerical workers believe that their jobs are temporary and that they will be rescued by marriage or some other windfall. And secretaries often identify with their bosses in a way that manual workers rarely do with their foremen. Many secretaries would consider it as an act of personal treason to join a union, which by its very nature has different objectives than management.

Anne Bogan, an executive secretary, expressed this classic identification: "I feel like I'm sharing somewhat of the business life of the men. So I think I'm much happier as the secretary to an executive than I would be in some woman's field, where I could perhaps make more money. But I wouldn't be an extension of a successful executive. I'm perfectly happy in my status."[17]

But times are changing. Women who relate only to a word processor do not feel particularly loyal to a boss, and women are beginning to realize that they will not be escaping from their desk for more than a few weeks or months during their adult life.

A new but rapidly spreading political movement is catching fire among clerical workers. The prototype of this movement is "9 to 5," the Boston organization of women office workers that came into being in 1973. Since then local organizations have sprung up in cities across the country, most of them now under the umbrella organization Working Women, National Organization of Office Workers. The goal of this organization is "to gain rights and respect for working women." This is a flexible approach that does not lock itself into the trap of equal rights. In the office worker's world there are few men with whom to achieve equality.

Working Women provides support for local groups by training organizers and helping with fund raising. It also sets national priorities, which may be displaced by local priorities. The first issues tackled by the national organization in the late seventies were the working conditions of women in banks—a gargantuan employer with notoriously low pay scales and little opportunity for women in management—and age dis-issues were displaced in the eighties by equal pay for crimination among all women office workers. These jobs of comparable worth, health and safety on the job, and reclassification of job titles.[18]

Office workers, like manual workers, have rarely taken the initiative to organize themselves. The most organized are those who work in the public sector and have been swept up by the wide net of city, state, or federal worker unions. In the private sector it is politically conscious professional women who have provided the catalyst. Baltimore Working Women (BWW), for instance, was born in a meeting of mainly professional women, already politically active (some socialist-feminists), who heard about the activities of 9 to 5 and believed that existing women's groups took little notice of clerical workers.

During the early stages of the BWW the professional women took the lead and helped raise funds from the national organization and other sources for a full-time staff member. They delayed elections and a formal organization until office workers themselves could be groomed for leadership.

The tactics of BWW have been imaginative and often rely on personal pressure rather than legal actions, which are expensive and seemingly endless. Then media are used effectively to make a point. In taking on the banking industry for failing to post promotional opportunities among the clerical staff, BWW publicly awarded the title "Miser of the Year" to a distinguished bank president. He was angry, but the postings soon appeared. To dramatize the unfair situation of older women workers, younger women read the older women's testimonies to a roomful of reporters.[19] They also provide practical information to their members on pension systems and how to file a sex-discrimination charge.

Working Women and its affiliates is not a labor union which is certified by the National Labor Relations Board and can enter into collective-bargaining negotiations with employers for wages and working conditions. The organization's focus is to raise the consciousness of office workers so that they can improve their condition through collective action of many forms, including the drive for comparable worth.

Comparable worth is a solution well suited to clerical

workers, since these jobs often require education and skills similar to better-paying male occupations. And clerical workers can be found in virtually every employment situation. There has been a great deal of opposition to comparing employees of two industries, or two governmental units. A secretary for a city government can be matched only against employees for that local government, and not be compared with employees in other government units, such as clerks in a federal tax office. Employers, when they are willing to recognize comparable worth (at this point, only public employers do), usually insist it apply only within one industry or unit.

Comparable worth is the hot idea of the eighties. Frightened away by the nonegalitarian nature of affirmative action, and discouraged by the meager results of Title VII discrimination actions, women have turned to an idea that is already old news in Europe. The basic concept of comparable worth is that workers should get equal pay for work of comparable worth. The hidden trap in this fine-sounding phrase is the meaning of worth. Is worth measured by its free-market value, or is it measured by the requirements and activities of the job itself?

Although it is by no means obvious that a secretary and a truck driver perform work of comparable worth, proponents claim there are job-evaluation tests based on skill levels, responsibilities, personal contacts, and working conditions which can determine equivalency. For instance, in the widely used Hay system, a supervisor of keypunch operators received a total of 268 points: 152 for knowhow, 50 for problem solving and 66 for accountability. The job receives 152 points for knowhow because the job classification requires advanced vocational training, the job is first-line supervision of a single function, and the job involves proficiency in human relations, since such skills are critical in motivating people at this level.[20]

Comparable worth is being hailed as the latest and greatest egalitarian solution. Its supporters claim that it comes under the twin umbrella of the Equal Pay for Equal Work Act of 1963 and Title VII, which prohibits not only individual discrimination in the workplace but patterns of discrimination, whether or not they are intentional. They insist that the fact that women are largely lumped in female occupations is the result of patterns of discrimination. Comparable worth would not take them out of these occupations, it would instead raise the level of pay to that of occupations dominated by men who perform comparable work.

In fact, comparable worth is *not* egalitarian in the spirit of Title VII and the Equal Pay Act, which set up a model to allow women to compete equally with men in male-dominated professions. It is antithetical to that model, since it keeps and protects women in female-dominated occupations by elevating their wages in these fields. Rather than encouraging women to compete with men, it encourages them to stay where they are and accept better pay.

This does not mean that comparable worth is not a useful weapon for women to improve their situations. For most women, there are good reasons why they are working where they are, above and beyond discrimination. The fact that female occupations provide more control over time and less physical or mental stress is usually the main determinant. Often the major problem with the female occupation is low pay. Staying put with better wages is more attractive to many women than bucking the working conditions of male occupations.

But comparable worth is in danger of being destroyed by the logic of its most avid advocates. By insisting that comparable worth is an egalitarian solution implied by

Title VII and the Equal Pay for Equal Work Act, rather than the protective idea it really is, its proponents set it up as an easy target to be cut down by the courts. Thus far the federal court decisions have been contradictory and confusing and have shown a general desire to duck this controversial issue.

In 1983, Jack Tanner, a federal district court judge in Washington State, severely shocked employers across the country by declaring that the state had discriminated against its workers in those jobs held mostly by women, and ordering an immediate 31 percent pay raise for twelve thousand women employees.[21] State officials claimed this would cost the taxpayers $800 million dollars.

An appeal was immediately filed with the Ninth Circuit federal court, and comparable-worth watchers, who now included millions of concerned women and frightened employers, waited anxiously for the Ninth Circuit's decision. The Ninth Circuit reversed Tanner's decision, stating that "Washington State's decision to participate in the market system, thereby basing compensation on competitive market rather than on a theory of comparable worth, did not establish a discriminatory motive so as to demonstrate sex discrimination on a disparate-treatment theory under Title VII . . ."[22]

The court stated the obvious: Title VII was consistent with a competitive free-market approach where women could compete with men by seeking better-paying jobs in men's occupations, and it was not intended to protect women in female enclaves where no internal discrimination could be shown.

Women are finally discovering that competing with men in the free market is not doing them much good. For good and practical reasons the lives that most women lead do not permit them to compete with men even if they wished to. And yet they cannot accept their new role as lifelong workers with the low wages and lack of advancement that their female-dominated occupations offer.

The aftermath of the comparable-worth defeat at the bench of the Ninth Circuit offers hope. When the Washington State workers' union petitioned for a rehearing, the state began negotiations with the union based on the job-rating formulas used in the case before Judge Tanner was called in. The bargaining resulted in the state putting up $106 million the first year and an additional $10 million each year until 1992, while the union dropped its petition for rehearing. About 35,000 workers will receive salary increases. Clerk typists, for example, will receive a 25 percent boost in pay, and nurses, social caseworkers, librarians, and employees in a score of other female-dominated jobs will also get higher pay.[23]

Without being forced by the courts, dozens of state and local entities, pushed by unions and concerned local women's groups, have undertaken comparable-worth studies which rate all jobs by some kind of point system. California leads the way in municipalities which have voluntarily (following substantial union pressure) established new pay scales based on their comparable-worth studies. California promoters of comparable worth are helped by the passage of a law in 1981 (which has since been thoroughly stalled by the governor), which clearly states a policy of setting salaries on a comparable-worth classification for government jobs.[24]

It will probably be a very long time, if ever, before Susan's job as a word processor in a private law firm will be attacked by a comparable-worth analysis. Public-sector workers are far better organized than their counterparts in the private sector, and public entities do not have to pay the piper of profit and can afford to look to a different standard. Only when Susan is lured away to work for the city government because of its substantially higher pay scale will the managing partner decide that a reevaluation of the pay scale is in order. In the meanwhile approximately two out of five workers are employed by government at some level— state, federal, or local. This provides a good deal of fertile ground for the growth of comparable worth.

It is doubtful, given the current national political climate, that equal pay for comparable worth will be mandated by federal law. Although the federal government is by no means above tinkering with the free market, it currently takes a strong laissez-faire posture. Title VII is not threatening, because it does not challenge the existing price and wage structure.

But comparable worth can provide a tough club for the fledgling office-worker associations in the private sector. Although comparability of wages is not likely to be achieved in the immediate future, it may scare employers into other concessions. A bank may discreetly decide to give its tellers an extra week's vacation rather than face the threat of a reevaluation of jobs.

THE WOMEN'S PROFESSIONS

In most statistical portrayals of the work world, the percentage of women professionals is very high compared with men professionals. But this is not a new phenomenon created by the growing ranks of women lawyers and doctors; it is the same picture that we have been seeing throughout the twentieth century. The vast majority of those women professionals are, as they always have been, in the women's professions: teaching, nursing, and social work.

The women's professions not only share an overwhelming majority of women in their ranks but have other characteristics which distinguish them from the "male" professions such as medicine or law. The training of women in the women's professions is shorter, their status is less legitimated, they have a less specialized body of knowledge, they have less autonomy from supervision, and they most often work for a public employer. These professions are often referred to by sociologists as the "semi-professions," indicating their middle-ground status between ordinary employees and the "real" professionals—doctors and lawyers.

These professions used to be the top of the ladder for women. With the drive for equality with men, they no longer command top prestige. Educated, ambitious women, those who live to work, increasingly choose the "real" professions, for their greater status. Nineteen percent of all freshmen in 1970 said they intended to choose teaching as a career, but only 5 percent expressed that intention in 1982. Women who choose the women's professions still get satisfaction and a sense of identity from their work, but they are insecure in their status.

My college friend Sandy loved her job as a third-grade teacher. "I felt so wise, teaching about the fundamentals that adults forget, like where rain comes from and why the sun shines." She went back to graduate school in educational administration largely because she felt looked down upon by her professor husband's colleagues and their wives. At university social functions she hesitated to say what she did, considering it a small victory if no one asked her about herself. She accomplished this mainly by not talking at all.

After many years of study, interrupted by the birth of her son, she completed her Ph.D. and now holds an academic administrative post at a junior college. Sandy is not so sure she made the right choice. "I'm the only one in my family that has to work in the summer, and I miss the little kids. Dealing with the faculty and my impossible dean is no fun. I'm going to try to switch into teaching."

In addition to slipping status, "burnout" is a major factor in all the women's professions. Because they do not have the independence of male professionals, women professionals often feel they are captives of a mindless bureaucracy. They have chosen these professions to help people, and they are kept away from the people they are trying to help.

A nurse's job in a modern hospital resembles that of a taxi dispatcher. It is her job to translate the doctor's orders into action, usually by dispatching orderlies or nurse's aides to the patients' rooms. She must also keep track of the accounting and of the drugs. The head nurses rarely leave the nurses' station. One nurse commented, "Seventy-five percent of my time is spent kardexing orders. I feel like a robot . . . I get farther and farther away from patients every day."[25]

All of these women's professions suffer from lack of incentive and reward. The salary range is both low and narrow, and the top may be reached quickly. A woman may peak in ten years and spend the next thirty years of her working life on the same salary rung. A small number can work their way into administration, but then they remove themselves from the people they chose to help.

Demoralized by low status, limited autonomy, and lack of pay incentive, all of the women's professions, especially nursing and social work, suffer a huge drop-out rate. It is not clear where these dropouts go, but they feel they can no longer tolerate their chosen profession.

Sex discrimination and unequal treatment are not the problem, since men are in the minority in these professions. Some observers claim that men in women's professions get paid better and rise to higher positions; this is offered as evidence of unequal treatment. But women are also well represented in higher administrative posts, and many women shy away from administration because of longer hours and loss of contact with children or patients or clients.

And the women's professions offer many attractive features that most men's professions lack. It is hard to think of more important work than teaching children, caring for the sick, and helping the needy. The practice of law has its rewards, but it is not usually characterized as an humanitarian endeavor.

Women's professions also hold an advantage over men's professions in controlling both time and stress. A teacher's schedule is well suited to family life, and nurses can usually bend their working schedule around their home needs. Social work is less flexible, but at least it meets the minimal criterion of a forty-hour week. Stress is surely present in all of these professions, but there is less direct competition with other professionals, and certainly there are shorter hours than are endured in the male professions.

How can women preserve the positive features of the women's professions that make them attractive to women with family responsibilities, while gaining more of the status, independence, and pay incentive that are found in the men's professions?

The women's professions have a great head start over most other areas in which women work, in that they are already strongly organized and therefore women can often influence their working conditions through collective bargaining. The majority of women in these professions also work for public employers, a far easier bargaining opponent than private employers.

The main-line strategies of equal opportunity and equal pay for equal work are not fruitful in these female-dominated professions, and comparable worth is questionable. An official of the largest teachers' organization, the National Education Association, complained, "Comparable worth doesn't do us much good, because they only compare us to other employees in that district. In most towns that means firemen and policemen, and teachers don't do badly in terms of the hours they work." Nurses have had some success in comparable-worth reevaluations in the public sector, but not as much as the big winners, office workers.

The most important strategy that professional organizations can take is to upgrade their professions by raising the requirements for entry into the field, and by requiring rigorous continuing education. High entrance requirements, the secret of success in most male professions, would both reduce the competition and raise the quality of the professionals. This should in turn allow the professionals to demand higher salaries.

And pay raises that reflect higher performance on the job are critically needed. Seniority-based wages are the kiss of death to professional excellence. Pay must be based on merit and incorporated into a real career track. Unfortunately, the women's professions are viewed, as are all female occupations, as a temporary work stint sandwiched in between family obligations. The continuity of contemporary women in the workplace must be reflected in the career track.

The 1986 Carnegie Report, "A Nation Prepared:

Teachers for the 21st Century," presented national rec-
ommendations for teachers which could be extrapolated
to improve the quality of all the women's professions.
They included:

· A National Board for Professional Teaching Standards to establish high standards and to certify teachers who meet those standards.
· A Master's in Teaching degree, including internships and residencies in the schools.
· Teachers' salaries and career opportunities that are
competitive with those in other professions.
· Incentives for teachers related to schoolwide student performance.

WORKING TOWARD THE FUTURE

Women who work to live need all the help they can get.
They have two choices: to get out of their female-
dominated occupations and plunge into male occupations in order to achieve livable wages, or to stay in
their female enclaves and better their condition. Because women need to control their time and the level
of stress they experience on their job, the great majority
will probably stay in their jobs. This is not a bad fate
as long as they can earn a living wage with some hope
of salary advancement over time: the pay difference
between a brand-new typist and one who has been on
the same job for twenty years is often negligible.

In addition to higher wages, women who work to
live need the kinds of support that all working mothers
need: flex time, maternity leaves, family sick leaves,
family medical benefits, and more vacations; a two-

week annual vacation is cruelly short for women with families. And, of course, reliable, low-cost day care is a necessity.

And Why should private employers or public employers provide these expensive and disruptive special considerations for women? They will supply them because they need women workers. If all mothers who work to live left their jobs tomorrow, the economy would collapse. There are not enough men to put the pieces together again. Employers are happy if they can get women cheap, but they would still have to hire them if they were more expensive. The changes I advocate might cause some shift in the wealth of the country, but they would not radically disrupt the economy.

The argument that wages and benefits are controlled by a free-market economy makes little sense in a country where the minimum wage, the Civil Service Commission, and unions are major determinants of wages.

But women will get nothing unless they demand it and sometimes fight for it. Self-reliance is the key to success in a country where the laws are enforced according to the political whim of each administration.

There is no question that immediate gains are more likely in the public rather than the private sector. Governments at all levels, federal, state and local, have been fertile fields for unions and the primary arena for comparable-worth activity. Certainly the biggest advances for office workers are likely to come in the public sector.

At the same time that the public sector is showing new consideration, the private sector is belligerently digging in its heels. Unions have had their backs broken or have simply faded away. Some of the married women who have newly entered the labor market are employed in the public sector, but most are not. Most office workers, retail sales clerks, waitresses, and factory workers work for private employers. These employers will take advantage of the increasingly hostile public opinion toward unions to halt new organizing activities.

For most women in female-dominated occupations the best bet is a union or a professional association with clout to advocate a variety of tough strategies. Different strategies will work for different groups of workers.

For unskilled manual workers, old-fashioned union strategies of collective bargaining buttressed by the threat of strike are necessary. Union grievance committees can handle issues of sexual harassment and discrimination on the job. But first these workers must be unionized, and that will take all the help that organized middle-class women can give to start the process in motion. Unskilled manual workers who want to move into skilled jobs need even more help. They must begin by being directed into training or apprentice programs for skilled trades and then pushed forward under union affirmative-action timetables. These women must also break new ground in new skilled trades growing up in the service/information sector. Entering old manufacturing trades that are on the decline is courting unemployment.

Office workers, the biggest group, and other semi-skilled workers in the service sector have great opportunity. The combination of unions and comparable worth, particularly in the public sector, could provide rapid progress. The private sector will offer a long hard fight. Comparable worth will be fought bitterly, and the advent of unions in industries like banking or the law, which have been virtually untouched by unions, will be strongly opposed.

Women's professions, most obviously represented by teachers and nurses, have already come a long way, but have a long way to go. Although unions and collective bargaining are generally well established, this group has suffered deeply from the exodus of those women who live to work into the male-dominated professions. Lack of status and self-worth can be combated by increased professional development accompanied by higher pay and merit incentives. The current debate over national educational policy is focusing on raising the status of teachers as a major solution to the crisis in education. Better teachers will produce better-educated students.

Above all, women who work to live must come to accept themselves as lifelong, not temporary, workers. They will not be rescued by a husband as their mothers and grandmothers were. If they have a husband, their husband's job alone will no longer support their family. They must learn from an early age to band with other women to improve working conditions in their female occupations and to improve their skills and knowledge for further advancement.

8

THE INVISIBLE MAJORITY: REENTRY AND PART-TIME WORKERS

A critical fact that is rarely mentioned in discussions about working women is that fewer than half work full time, year round. It appears to be a closely held secret that most women workers are part-timers.[1] According to the very few studies of part-time workers, most women choose to work part time because they must balance family obligations, while many do so because they cannot find adequate child care, but the great majority would not choose the jobs they have. Women who work part time generally must accept low-status, low-skilled jobs with the accompanying unattractive features of low pay and no benefits. These women are not "pin money" workers whose husbands provide the necessities while they work for the luxuries. Most women work part time because they or their families need food, clothing, housing, and education.

Part-time work has been the fastest-growing component of the service economy of recent years, providing the illusion of a healthy economy producing ever more jobs and relentlessly reducing unemployment. The reality from an employee's point of view is not so healthy. A minimum wage and no medical or pension benefits are the typical conditions of employment.

Reentry women are by definition those women who return to the labor force after a long absence, usually spent raising a family. Reentry and part-time women share the bottom level of the labor market. Many reentry women are part-time workers, both by choice and by chance. But even when they are full-time workers, they have a hard time climbing toward better jobs at higher pay.

Reentry and part-time workers include women who work to live and women who formerly lived to work. Rarely do you find them in the higher echelons of the male-dominated high-status occupations. Women who start on the fast track and then drop out are not likely to be allowed reentry into the race.

These women are the invisible majority. They have no voice of their own, and no one to speak for them. They have been ignored by the women's movement, by unions, by everyone. They need special consideration in getting and holding jobs. They don't need the right to compete with men. They need jobs that provide a decent living and benefits.

For most, their marginal condition is caused by the obligations of motherhood that they took on. If they are still mothering, they need help to make their work life possible. If the brunt of their burden has passed, they need help to catch up. These women also need special consideration in accumulating Social Security and private pensions so that they will not end their days destitute, as many women do. Instead they are penalized for the years they spend out of the job market raising children. A Social Security system and private pension plans set up for a male model of continuous work with ever higher earnings guarantees a bleak old age for these women.

RE-ENTRY SHOCK

Fay Dalucci fell through a large hole in the mythical safety net that is supposed to protect Americans from destitution. When she was fifty, her husband of thirty years walked off and the courts awarded her one half of the few thousand dollars netted from the sale of the family home, and no alimony. Fay was not eligible for unemployment, since she had not worked in twenty-five years. She was not eligible for welfare, since she no longer had dependent children and was not physically disabled. As a divorced wife she would be eligible for about a third of her husband's Social Security retirement benefits, but only when he retired, which would not be for at least fifteen years.

Fay became a reluctant reentry woman. With three years of college and some office-work experience twenty-five years ago, she was turned down for the first five office jobs she applied for and lost courage to apply for any more. She was certain she was unemployable and felt grateful when she was offered a part-time counter job in a bakery, which offered no medical benefits and no sick leave.

"After I paid rent, I had almost nothing left for food,"

she says, "so I lived on the day-old goods that they couldn't sell. I was afraid to dip into my bank account, afraid I'd get sick."

Fay is a casualty of the climate of opinion that accepts divorce at whim and maintains that women can take care of themselves. Although Fay would like to take care of herself, she needs help to do so. Her years of child-raising have left her at a great disadvantage. Sex discrimination is not her problem, since she is competing only against other women in female occupations. Age discrimination is a factor, but this proves to be a slippery charge, since an employer will never admit to it, and Fay's long absence from the job market compared to younger women applicants can be used as a plausible excuse. Very few women in Fay's position would have the courage to bring a complaint to the Equal Employment Opportunity Commission (EEOC) office under the Age Discrimination Act contained in the Employment Act of 1967. And if they did, they would have a nearly impossible burden to prove their charge.

It is difficult to know for sure how many women are in Fay's shoes, but in 1975 there were 4.5 million divorced or separated women and only 4 percent received alimony. In that same year, according to the U.S. census, there were 1.6 million widowed, divorced, or separated women between thirty-five and sixty-four who fell below the official poverty line.[2] Fay with her part-time job and small savings probably would make the cut; she would not be numbered among the official poor.

As a displaced homemaker Fay belongs to a class of women that has gotten a good deal of media attention but very little actual public support. The major government retraining program, CETA (Comprehensive Employment and Training Act), as restructured in 1978, mentioned displaced homemakers as a target group, but made the eligibility requirement a below-poverty-level income and a long period of unemployment. Women who had not been in the labor market (and therefore were not considered unemployed) or who were slightly above the rock-bottom income requirements missed this boat.[3] CETA was abolished in 1983 and replaced by the very limited Job Training Partnership Act. In general, governmental retraining efforts have focused on young men, with the expectation that this group would have the longest productive work life.

On the positive side, women who wish to reenter the job market, because of divorce, a mortgage to meet, or an empty nest, can find many counseling and support groups, if no real jobs. Almost all community and four-year colleges have offered programs for reentry women, and a variety of church and community organizations offer classes or counseling as well. It has become possible for older women to return to school without the stigma of having the only gray or graying head in an English-literature classroom. But it is not easy to get the kind of training that produces marketable skills.

The media have picked up on the forty-year-old woman law student or the thirty-five-year-old woman medical student—but this is mostly media fluff. Few women can pursue the education they might have taken up if they were eighteen or twenty-one. Starting law school or medical school in midlife, especially if there are children at home, is an unrealistic option for most middle-aged women. Their economic needs are more immediate. Even completing a deserted B.A. will not provide the kinds of quickly marketable skills that get jobs.

The women who do return to college to get that degree or advanced degrees are usually married women with no pressure for immediate employment. They can afford to take years, if necessary, without concern for an immediate payoff. When and if these women return to work, they can choose to take part-time or occasional work without regard to a living wage.

The road to attaining employable skills is often long and rocky, as it was for one of my students, Mary Clare. On Christmas Eve, 1979, Mary Clare's husband called and said he had to work late. Three days later, a florist's bill arrived at the house for two dozen roses delivered to her husband's secretary's home on Christmas Eve. For Mary Clare, this was the beginning of a three-year nightmare which included a twenty-four-hour commitment to the psychiatric ward followed by a year of continuous migraine headaches and suspected cancer.

That Christmas Eve was not the first indication that her marriage was failing. Several years before, her husband had begun a love affair with computers that came to absorb him completely, leaving little room for his wife or their two small daughters. At that time Mary Clare, fearing the collapse of her marriage, quietly began to investigate the job market. With two years of college and minimal work experience, she was offered only minimum-wage file-clerk jobs. She tried a stint as a nursery-school aide. She both hated the job and recognized, with some relief, that it would never support her. She decided to join her husband and took evening courses in computer programming which promised a better financial future. They spent Sundays together working on their computer programs, which Mary Clare came to loathe. "For him it was the best of times," she recalled, "for me it was the worst."

To her husband's scorn, she dropped computer programming and did nothing until what she most feared occurred: her husband left her to live with his secretary. Her complicated divorce settlement effectively allowed her to live in her house with her small daughters for a few years while forcing her to use up her half of the equity for support. Finally propelled by the panic of necessity, Mary Clare went to her local junior college for counseling and was steered into an X-ray-technician course because it promised good job prospects. From the beginning Mary Clare disliked everything about it. She had no interest in the technical material she was forced to learn and began developing ever more severe migraine headaches, until they numbered twenty or more each month with only brief respites in between. She eventually became completely bedridden and was diagnosed (improperly) as having an inoperable pituitary tumor.

I met Mary Clare when she had begun a turnaround to improvement at age forty-two. Refusing to listen to her doctor's death sentence, she tried other doctors within and outside the medical establishment and finally found relief with an acupuncturist. She was tentatively trying other training routes and enrolled as a student in the paralegal program which I had founded with re-entry women in mind. During the course of eighteen months, I observed Mary Clare gain skills and confidence and lose eighty pounds. She landed a half-time job at a nonprofit agency while still a student and is now preparing to interview for a full-time job as a paralegal.

"I am very excited about being self-sufficient," she confided, "but I have fears about where I will live and the style I will live in."

Over the past ten years I have counseled hundreds of reentry women who are seeking employment skills. They come in many forms, from thirty-five-year-old former teachers whose children are now in school all day to fifty-five-year-old women whose marriages have ended, leaving them on the short side of subsistence. Some have a college degree or graduate work plus substantial work experience. Others married in their teens and became full-time mothers. Their motivations for wanting to return to the full-time job market vary somewhat, but money to support themselves and/or their families is surely paramount. Divorce is the immediate catalyst for many of these women, since they cannot afford to take a low-paying part-time job and need retraining to find employment that pays a living wage.

Whatever their age or background, there is a predictable pattern of reentry that virtually all women experience. But not all make it through the complete pattern; there are many possibilities for dropping out along the way.

STAGE ONE: THE WANT ADS

No matter what they have done before they dropped out of the job market to raise children, virtually all women experience a severe crisis of confidence when they consider reentry.

Many women, like Mary Clare, begin with a tentative search through the want ads. Few women have the courage to aim as high as their last job. If a woman was formerly an account executive for an advertising agency, she is most likely to apply for a job as copywriter. If she was an administrative assistant, she will look at the ads for secretary.

When the want ads produce no interviews, a public employment agency is often the next step in their search. Too often their worst fears are supported. A thirty-two-year-old divorced woman with a bachelor's degree had the following discouraging experience:

"I got one suggestion from a man at the State Employment Agency that really knocked me out. I had gone to him, about getting a job in the art field, and he said, 'Here's one. This is a great job. You could make five or six dollars an hour. Weighing noodles at the airport. And it's not taxing at all.' I said, 'You don't understand. I want to be taxed. I want to do something that's hard. I don't want to sit there like I've had a lobotomy and make six dollars an hour.' That was the low point, especially when I considered doing it."[4]

The majority of reentry women are looking for sales or clerical jobs, but a disproportionately small percentage of employers list with public agencies, guaranteeing the job-seeker a high rate of failure. Public agencies rarely offer testing or counseling. In a study of public employment agencies in twenty representative cities, it was found that only 20 percent of all job applicants were counseled at all, and only 15 percent were tested in any fashion.[5]

On the other hand, a private agency, especially one where the fee is paid by the employer, will often politely but pointedly reject the older reentrant as not being quite right for its clientele. The reentrant will understand immediately that she is too old and unattractive, and feel embarrassed that she has taken the agency's precious time.

If the reentrant is actually offered a job, no matter how far below her skills or salary requirements, she may accept out of gratitude and relief. Most reentry women do not get beyond this limited job search. Some, like Fay Dalucci, accept any job, even one that does not support them, because they do not have the confidence to believe they can do any better. Others, like Mary Clare, retreat back into the house following an unsuccessful foray into the job market.

STAGE TWO:
SEEKING MARKETABLE SKILLS

When Mary Clare was finally pushed out of the house by divorce, she sought help. The first place she contacted was Displaced Homemakers, a nonprofit organization to aid older women who are victims of divorce, which she had read about in the newspaper. They said her eleven-year marriage had been too short to qualify her as a displaced homemaker, but sent her on to the local junior college. This college had an active women's center; although most of the women were twenty years her junior, there were several who looked like age peers. A counselor at the college performed a short evaluation of her skills and gave her a standardized preference test. This counselor advised that she definitely needed training and insisted that the field most appropriate and most employable was X-ray technology. Mary Clare was skeptical, but she needed help and felt powerless to object. Facing her first homework assignment, she looked at the technical material on the page and felt a tremendous headache.

Many reentry women find that counselors direct them to training programs strictly on the basis of employability rather than the woman's own aptitude, interest, or even prior skills and training. Although finding a job must be a primary goal, it can be agony to enter a field for which you have no aptitude or liking.

"I told her I hated computers, and finally I had to purposely flunk the computer aptitude test so that she would not force me into computer programming." This complaint was offered by Marie, a black woman who had served as a policewoman for six years until she was severely injured trying to restrain a violent criminal suspect high on PCB. Since she was physically unable to return to police work, the state was obliged to retrain her. "I had done all my college in criminology and the law, and law was what I really cared about. They didn't care, they just wanted to get rid of me."

Reentry women are caught in a double bind. Only by training or retraining can they gain the skills that will help them gain a good job, but the economic pressures that force them into the job market make the process of retraining a luxury they can ill afford. Not only do they forgo a salary during these school days, they must take on additional expenses. Even the junior-college systems, which are free in most states, charge for books; and of course there are transportation, lunch, and incidentals.

Many of the best training programs which promise good employability are run by private colleges or proprietary schools where a $5,000-plus annual tuition charge is common. Although many schools and colleges have encouraged reentry women to apply, they rarely provide any special scholarships. Often reentry women find that they are not eligible for student loans because they own a house or part of a house, although they may have little or no income. If they have a working husband there is very little hope for financial aid.

The fortunate reentry woman who conquers the financial obstacles and makes it back into the classroom to gain marketable skills often feels like a six-year-old on her first day of school. Her hiatus from education destroys any self-confidence she had as a young student; and she may not have felt very confident when she was young. The advantage she has over young students and over her own youth, for that matter, is raw determination. She cannot afford to fail.

The new student must make serious adjustments in her home life as well. Lillian Rubin, in her book *Women of a Certain Age: The Midlife Search for Self,* describes the great risk that married women take by destroying the equilibrium of an old marriage. A new student but old wife feels that she must give herself to her studies: "I tell him to go to the movies himself. After all, you can't talk there. So why can't he go sit in the dark by himself? Why does he need me for that? But he won't. He just hangs around and sulks, and then I feel so guilty I have a hard time studying anyhow."[6]

Although usually much poorer, divorced women do not suffer the tension of a neglected spouse: "Let me tell you, it's much easier to go to school when you're divorced, even when you have children, than it is when you're married. At least it was for me. I couldn't possibly have gone to school seriously—I mean for a degree—when I was married. When you are divorced, you just have much more control over your own life and your time."[7]

STAGE THREE: THE JOB

If a reentry woman has made a good choice in the field and the training program she has pursued, there will be jobs when she finishes her training and she will receive help in finding one. If she has made a bad choice she will find herself competing for a small number of jobs against more experienced workers and younger trainees. Older reentry women must compete with the population bulge known as the Baby Boom which produced too many bodies for too few jobs. Many women in fields such as real estate, financial management, and even computer programming find they have spent months or even years training for a job they cannot get.

But for the woman who has chosen appropriately, there will be a job. Many employers have seen the wisdom of hiring a mature woman with better organizational skills and fewer family commitments.

The paralegal field, which I know well, has been kind to reentry women. Partly because it is a new field, it has no firm stereotype of what age a paralegal should be, and the job market has expanded fairly rapidly. Following a relatively short training period (programs vary between three months and two years) a reentry woman can find an interesting job in a stimulating environment. Although the work varies widely, most paralegals spend time preparing cases for trial, communicating with clients and witnesses, and carrying out a wide variety of legal tasks under the supervision of a lawyer. They perform little or no typing and hold a status somewhere between the legal secretary and the young associate. A paralegal will typically work for a private law firm, often in an attractive office.

But paralegals share the fate of all workers in female-dominated fields. The salary, which is not much better than a beginning legal secretary's to begin with, is barely livable for a single person, and career advancement is limited. While law offices have a clear career track for the young lawyers (usually up or out), many regard paralegals as temporary workers. "Our girls will either go to law school or get married in two years," commented the administrator for one of the largest San Francisco law firms. Their forty-five- or fifty-year-old "girls" are not likely to do either. What they are usually forced to do is jump from firm to firm to slightly improve their situation. This results in a lot of wasted time and effort on the part of both employer and employee.

And when the employed reentry woman starts to look down the road to retirement she is frightened by what she sees. If she is depending upon her own wages for

Social Security she is penalized for having dropped out to raise children. Social Security benefits are based on average lifetime earnings, and they drop out only the lowest five years. All those years more than five that she stayed at home to raise children will be averaged as a zero. If her new job has a private pension plan her relatively short period of contributions will yield a pittance to live on.

FUTURE PROSPECTS

Ironically, it is the middle-aged reentry woman who has the most to give to the work force and yet has the least chance of advancement. A woman in her middle years may have twenty to thirty years of continuous work life, with decreasing or no home responsibilities. She may, in fact, feel able to work longer hours and take on more stress than she could in her child-raising years. Most women at age forty-five claim they feel physically as strong and mentally more organized than they were at twenty. They have developed better focus and greater motivation.

The two greatest obstacles for reentry women are their own lack of confidence and a marketplace that doesn't know what to do with them. Clearly all reentry women need specific job counseling, and probably 90 percent or more need retraining or serious brushing up.

There are some fields, like nursing or teaching, where it is possible for a reentry woman to brush up on old skills and reenter the field, although usually at a lower level than where she left it. There are other fields, usually the male-dominated fields, where she is not welcome to reenter at all. The career clock does not make allowances for dropping out and stepping back in. In law, for instance, it is possible to maintain a bar membership and to brush up on the changes that have occurred, but it is very difficult to find someone to hire a woman who has been out of the field for over ten years. This is true as well for high-level corporate jobs, and for nearly all male-dominated professions which follow a male model of career progress. Sometimes it is impossible for women to make use of their past skills at all, no matter how sophisticated.

For most women reentering the working world, previous education and skills are not marketable without significant retraining. A twenty-year-old B.A. in English literature followed by a stint as an editor for a large publisher has little cash value years later. A woman with previous experience as a secretary has a better chance of getting a job immediately.

Betty Friedan in *The Second Stage* recommends a CETA-like approach which combines formal training with incentives to employers to hire the trainees and provide further on-the-job training. This would be particularly useful in some of the newer high-tech areas such as data processing and word processing. It would also work with the more traditional skills of bookkeeping, typing, and cashiering. All the semiskilled areas of the service sector which have sought women could easily absorb properly trained older women.

In women's professions such as teaching and nursing, the unions and the professional associations could take an affirmative role in helping women reenter. They could provide refresher courses and put pressure on employers, through either collective bargaining or friendly persuasion, to give special consideration to reentry women.

The male-dominated professions and corporate management are the hardest to crack. Here the male model of continuous participation in the workplace and a steady ascent to greater responsibility and greater riches serves as a barrier to middle-aged reentrants. Most of the jobs are outside the reach of unions and are in the private rather than the public sector. But in most of these fields women have developed their own professional associations. Up to this point they have used them as a forum to share problems they have encountered in climbing the ladder to success, but they could use the organizations as an effective lobby to provide alternate career ladders. The ability to reenter without forgoing years of hard-won experience should be a major concern for all women in male-dominated fields. Here also, women's organizations could provide refresher courses to help older women climb back into the field.

Affirmative action is implicit in all of these solutions. Affirmative action for reentry women in most fields does not mean asking for preference over men because of patterns of past discrimination, but instead means recognizing the experience and maturity that older women offer as a special asset over younger workers; most often these younger workers will be women. Employers can be convinced that it is in their best interest to hire women who have more to give to work because they are needed less at home. With CETA-like training programs employers can be given the incentive of a subsidized training period to sweeten the deal.

Social Security reform and pension reform are also special concerns of reentry women. Women should be rewarded, not punished, for the years they spend raising children. It should be public policy to treat these years as paid labor in determining Social Security income. Private pension plans should allow older women workers to "catch up" by increased contributions on both sides, in order that they may receive a decent retirement income.

The problems of reentry women are beginning to be addressed by struggling individual groups, but not by the nation as a whole, which is focused on the young woman with the attaché case. Displaced Homemaker Centers, pioneered by the Displaced Homemakers Project, a nonprofit organization which began in Oakland, California, in 1975, have spread rapidly through the country. These centers reach out to the woman who "has been displaced from her role as a homemaker through widowhood, divorce or separation, and can no longer depend on the income of another family member for her livelihood." They provide support, counseling, referrals to public agencies, and outreaches to private industry for job placement.[8]

The Older Women's League, begun by Tish Somers, grew out of the Displaced Homemakers Project in 1978. OWL, as the group is popularly known, has established an effective presence in Washington to lobby for the special concerns of older women. Jobs for older women has been one of their targets, as has wider Social Security coverage, equity in private pensions, health insurance, and caregiver support services.

But these tiny organizations cannot begin to take on all the problems of all reentry women, and they do not attempt to do so. Only a strong public commitment can provide the massive retraining that would make reentry women job ready. Only a concerted political drive will force the necessary changes in the health care and Social Security and pension regulations which would provide a decent old age for women who start later in life.

In the area of pension reform a glimmer of hope has been offered by the passage of the Retirement Equity Act of 1984. This act enables at least some women to receive retirement benefits who were previously ineligible. Specifically, workers can now participate in pension plans at the age of twenty rather than twenty-five; pension plans must count the years of service from the time a person turns eighteen instead of twenty-two; employees who have worked fewer than five years may take up to five years off without losing pension credit for earlier service; and pension plans may not be permitted to count a one-year maternity or paternity leave as a break in service. The law dictates that widows and widowers are eligible for some benefits even if their spouse dies before retirement age. It also requires the written permission of the spouse before a worker can waive survivor benefits for the spouse.[9]

PART-TIME WORKERS: THE BOTTOM OF THE BARREL

The majority of women workers are part-time workers, and they all have at least three things in common: they are underpaid, they are underemployed for the skills and education they possess, and they are ignored by organized women, by labor unions, by public policymakers, and even by one another. Most part-time women workers think of themselves as in transition toward a full-time job, usually in a different field, or en route to leaving the work force entirely. They tend to consider their unsatisfactory work condition like a cold: unpleasant, but livable with, and bound to pass. They do not consider this temporary work as part of their permanent identity, and therefore they are not willing to make major efforts to alter it.

The persistent myth about women part-time workers is that they are working for "pin money," the fur coat or the season ticket to the opera. The reality is that due to the combination of the breakdown of the family wage system and the rise of the mother-headed household, the majority of part-time workers need the money for the basic necessities. Part-time work enables many mothers without husbands to keep their families off the welfare rolls.

There has been an explosion of part-time work in the low-paying wholesale and retail trade and service industries, and an even greater explosion of women seeking part-time work. Debbie is a good example of this. Debbie was a teacher, but there are no teaching jobs available near her home (she would have to commute fifty miles each way for a job), and she has two small children, one not yet in kindergarten. Debbie and her husband stretched their budget to buy a modest house, and with inflation they feared they would lose it. Some months they must dig into their small savings to pay the mortgage. Debbie cannot become a substitute teacher, since she needs advance warning, which substitutes rarely have, in order to find a baby-sitter. Most other daytime jobs would not pay enough to cover the baby-sitter.

Debbie has chosen to work the seven-to-eleven shift four nights a week at the 7–11 store near her home. She gets slightly more than minimum wage, but her husband baby-sits. "We get some really weird types here at night, but I don't mind," she says. "Since I don't get out much during the day it is kind of entertaining." Debbie takes her low-skilled, low-paying job with equanimity because she doesn't feel she has much choice and she doesn't think she will be doing it forever.

Part-time work is the great leveler. The same low-level jobs and low-level pay are open to women almost regardless of their background and education. Women work part time in all the fields where women work full time, but with significant differences. While 12.6 percent of all full-time women work in professional and technical fields, only 6 percent work part time in these fields, and these are at the lowest end financially.[10] Their jobs are likely to be nonprofessional or quasi-professional in nature. The jobs performed may not even be related to the profession. A part-time nurse may serve as a receptionist, and a part-time lawyer may function as a paralegal or a law clerk.

Clerical work attracts the same percentage of full-time and part-time women workers (about 45 percent), but the big discrepancy occurs with sales, where only 19 percent of all workers are women and 15 percent of these are part-time workers.[11] Women do not hold the high-paying corporate sales jobs. They are found in the long-on-your-feet jobs at the department store in the local shopping mall, or selling makeup door to door.

More than one-third of all women agricultural workers are part-time workers, called out for the harvest and sent back for the slack times in between. More than one-third of all workers in food stores, drugstores, eating and drinking establishments, real estate, private households, and religious and nonprofit membership organizations are part-time workers, while only 3 percent of federal civil-service employees are part time.[12]

Not only do part-time workers get paid considerably less than their full-time counterparts, who are usually also women, but they get no consideration regarding work schedules, and usually no health insurance, pension coverage, or sick leave. It is ironic that many welfare mothers who would like to work part time in order to increase their income are prevented from doing so because they would jeopardize their rights to free medical care under Medicaid.

Why don't these women simply move into full-time work, where, if nothing else, the pay is higher? Some would like to move in this direction but are held back by the absence of full-time jobs, lack of transportation, or, as in agricultural labor, an industry that is part time in nature. But the overwhelming reason is that most women who work part time do so because they have family responsibilities which they believe cannot be combined with full-time work. For some women it is simply impossible to find adequate low-cost child care. Other women believe that raising children is a more important priority than a full-time job, no matter what the cost.

The irony is that most women with children who work full time yearn for the relative freedom of part-time work, while part-time workers want the salary and benefits of full-time workers. Surveys of working women regularly verify that full-time working mothers believe a work week of twenty to thirty hours would greatly improve the frantic quality of their everyday lives, but they simply cannot afford the drastic cut in pay or often cannot bear the kind of work that is available to them.

Clearly the elevation of part-time jobs to make the pay and benefits proportionately comparable to their full-time counterparts and the creation of permanent part-time jobs that use the education and skills of the worker should be a goal for all women workers. But, surprisingly, it is an almost nonexistent issue. Even women themselves hold the belief that women work part time for "the extras"—that if they really needed the money they would get a full-time job.

The requirement of full-time workers in most workplaces is a tradition rather than a necessity. A woman orthopedist in a group practice could certainly see patients three days rather than five days a week, but this is not allowed in most HMOs. A woman lawyer who specializes in medical malpractice could do the same. Most clerical jobs, with the exception of a personal secretary, could be filled by more than one person or could be adjusted to suit a part-time schedule. Assembly-line work is measured in shifts rather than weeks. Cooperative job-sharing where the individuals work together to develop a consistent policy and style could work in most administrative posts.

Part-time workers are often more productive and efficient. Since their time is limited, they push to get the job done. They suffer less from job burnout and boredom than their full-time counterparts.

But tradition dies hard and employers know they are getting a good deal by paying part-time workers low salaries and no benefits. In many private pension funds employees who work less than nineteen hours each week do not have to be covered by pensions at all. Part-time workers can be laid off by whim and rarely acquire any seniority rights.

There are a few hopeful movements toward recognition of permanent, full-status part-time workers. Some teachers' unions, albeit with a great deal of controversy, have introduced the concept of permanent, even tenured part-time positions in a few colleges. The tradition is more firmly established in many secondary and primary schools. The federal government, in the 1978 Part-Time Employment Act, created a potential career track for part-time employees, but this potentially favorable move has been largely aborted by the relentless human-services budget cuts of the eighties.

The part-time option must be pursued on several fronts. Federal legislation which mandates private pensions and at least partial health coverage for regular part-time workers who work a minimum of ten hours a week is a good start. But the main force of the attack must be taken up by unions in collective bargaining, by professional associations such as the state bars, and by all variety of women's groups who have an interest in meaningful part-time work for mothers—which should be all women's groups, period.

9

WOMEN'S RIGHTS
AND
WOMEN'S VISIONS

To empower the present we must have a vision of the future. I fear that the present trajectory of women's lives is aiming toward a bleak future.

I see my daughter Eve, now seven, and her generation living alone most of their adult lives in small, efficiency apartments. There are few children in this dreary vision. Women have given up on having children, not because they have committed themselves to career, but because they have learned too well from my generation that a woman cannot depend upon marriage to last the duration of child-raising. They have learned that mothers get stuck with an exhausting burden of work at home and in the marketplace. Boys, in turn, have learned from their fathers' generation that having children means awkward weekend visits and fights about support payments.

This sad trajectory seems to be already in place. Between 1970 and 1987 the percentage of Americans who are married with children under eighteen plummeted from 40.3 percent of the population to 27.5 percent. The number of adults who live alone rose from 17.1 percent to 23.6 percent.[1]

In my dark vision, men and women still give marriage a try once, twice, or more, but they have lost the touch for long-term commitment. Work, not family, has become the focus of their lives. Most women, unburdened by children, are definitely doing better in the marketplace relative to men. But in fact the average wage continues to slide downward in the relentlessly low-paying service/information sector, and men and women alike find it increasingly difficult to support even themselves. Status is measured in clothes and cars rather than in the big-ticket items of homes and second homes, affordable only to the very well off.

I fear that the egalitarian strategy, which pits women against men, is already helping to produce my dark vision of isolated individuals with limited human ties. And it is the handmaiden of an economic trend which promises ever more jobs at ever lower salaries. I fear a life of material and emotional impoverishment for my children.

But this vision is not yet certain. We do have the power to affect the future by changing the present. In a brighter vision, Eve and her generation have come to terms with the pattern of women's lives. As young women they stretch and challenge themselves, realistically preparing for a lifetime of both work and family. As mothers they turn their energies more toward their children, and in midlife, with children grown, they take up worldly tasks with full energy and full recognition. In this optimistic view of the future, men and women have reached an understanding about commitment, about sharing the load, about long-term loving. Divorce is no longer considered the accepted solution to all marital problems.

A vision of a future in which family and work are gracefully integrated over the span of a woman's life requires a change of heart as well as mind. Family and children must be valued and promoted. Moral responsibility must be reintroduced into the marriage contract.

A rejuvenated women's-rights strategy could begin by drawing together women on the left, the right and the middle of the political spectrum who agree that divorce is damaging the lives of millions of women and children. The cold statistic that women alone with children are six times as likely to fall below the poverty line as are married couples surely provides a politically neutral rallying call. The stunning fact that more than half of our children will spend at least part of their lives in a single-parent household should be a call to arms.

Abortion, the powerfully divisive issue about which women will never agree, has obscured the fact that there are central issues about which women do agree. Protection of children, a reversal of the relentless rise in divorce, sustaining a good material standard for family life: these are goals around which all women can join.

The home, however, is now only half of a woman's life. One clear fact presents itself in all my visions of the future: my daughter, along with her peers, will spend virtually all her adult life in the work force. She may take short breaks for childbirth, and if she is lucky she may work less than full time during her child-rearing years, but she will not have the option of being a full-time housewife. The role that was required in her grandmother's generation and looked down upon in my generation will wither away in her generation.

It is the necessity of lifelong work outside the home that renders all previous models of women's lives obsolete and begs for new solutions to new problems. History offers us some long-term guidelines as to values and priorities, but we must invent practical strategies for getting through the day.

Arrangements at work must complement arrangements at home to make up a life that is workable, not just exhausting. Women's rights in the workplace must focus on a higher minimum wage and fairly paid, fully benefited jobs which make accommodation to the needs of women workers with children. All working mothers need reliable, government-subsidized child care and after-school care. They also need paid maternity leaves, additional family sick leave, and good medical and pension benefits. Many working mothers could take advantage of flex time and regularized part-time work. These guidelines prevail whether a woman is a doctor or a word processor.

These demands are not unrealistic; they are simply requesting necessary everyday improvements in women's lives. But how can women expect to change the fundamental conditions of their family and work lives at a time when government is steadily shrinking away from regulating the marketplace and from providing basic social benefits for those who need them? The answer is strong organization and pressure on appropriate officials and institutions. Change occurs, as it always has occurred in America, when enough people push hard enough in the same direction.

The push for women's rights must come at local, state, and federal levels and from both private and public sectors. Divorce, custody, day care, tax relief for parents, part-time jobs, and medical benefits for women and children must become issues upon which all candidates for local, state, and federal government are forced to take a stand. Geraldine Ferraro, the first woman to run for Vice President, pointedly did not address women's issues in her campaign. "I wanted people to vote for me not because I was a woman," she says, "but because they thought I would make the best Vice President."[2]

Candidates for office must *not* be allowed to duck women's-rights issues. All candidates and political parties must be as forthright regarding their positions on women's rights as they are on nuclear arms or water pollution. The ERA was easy because it required no more than lip service. It was a statement of principle; politicians did not have to allocate money or set up expensive programs. Women's rights will require politicians to put their money where their mouth is. Child care and medical benefits cost money. Changes in tax laws to benefit working parents will have fiscal impact.

Change in the workplace will occur only through tough bargaining. Tight organization in the form of professional associations or unions must force through changes in salaries and conditions of work. Comparable-worth and affirmative-action initiatives are most successful if pushed for by organized workers. Federal and state laws can give support in terms of mandating pension and medical benefits and maternity or caretaker leaves, but bread-and-butter issues must be fought for within the industry or profession.

Women who are well organized must take up the task of organizing those who are not, as previous generations of women before them have done. Feminist organizations like NOW and NWPC can broaden their focus from those at the top to those who need help at the bottom. Teachers and nurses, well schooled in union tactics, can help their sisters who are clerical workers or

manual workers to develop the consciousness to organize themselves. The vast numbers of new jobs offered
in the service sector are low paid because the workers
are poorly organized.

The American tradition is to fix things only after
they have broken down, not to plan for the future. It
was not until the Depression of the 1930s had brought
the nation to its economic knees that the federal government responded with full-scale relief and a new
economic direction. More than the economy is in trouble today. The bleak future of the American family and
the shrinking resources for the American worker call
for all the imagination and planning that America can
muster.

A broad-based women's-rights agenda will work for
men as well as women. The emotional consequences of
divorce and separation from children are devastating
to men as well as to women. The slipping wage in the
growing service sector affects the paychecks of the
ever larger numbers of men who work there as well
as women.

A vision of the future must concentrate on quality
of life, not equality between the sexes.

NOTES

1. THE EQUALITY TRAP

1. Victor R. Fuchs, "Sex Differences in Economic Well-Being," *Science* 232 (Apr. 1986), p. 460.
2. The 70 percent figure is reported in "Money Income and Poverty Studies in Families in the U.S., *Current Population Reports* (Washington, D.C.: Bureau of the Census, 1987). The 1939 figure is reported in Sylvia Hewlett, *A Lesser Life* (New York, 1985), p. 71.
3. Frank Levy, "Actually We Are All Getting Poorer," *New York Times*, May 3, 1987.
4. Lenore J. Weitzman, *The Divorce Revolution* (New York, 1985).
5. Lenore J. Weitzman, "The Economics of Divorce: Social and Economic Consequences of Property, Alimony and Child Support Awards," *UCLA Law Review* 28 (1981), p. 1251.
6. *Newsweek*, July 15, 1985, p. 43.
7. *Business Week*, Jan. 28, 1985.

8. Michael Moore, "We Are the Baby Bust," *San Francisco Chronicle*, Mar. 1, 1987.

9. Robert Pears, "U.S. Reports Decline in Infant Mortality," *New York Times*, Mar. 16, 1983.

10. Report of the California Commission on the Status of Women, 1985.

11. As quoted in *Ms.*, July 1986, p. 48.

12. *Ibid.*, p. 48.

13. *Ibid.*, p. 87.

14. This interview, as well as all of the other personal interviews in this book, has been altered in terms of the names and some of the details of identity in order to preserve anonymity.

15. *New York Times*, Feb. 22, 1986, p. 48.

16. Barbara Ehrenreich, *The Hearts of Men: American Dreams and the Flight from Commitment* (New York, 1983), p. 121.

17. *Ibid.*, p. 12.

18. Colette Dowling, *The Cinderella Complex* (New York, 1981), pp. 5–14.

19. Andrew Hacker, "Farewell to the Family," *New York Review of Books*, Mar. 18, 1982, p. 37.

20. Carl Degler, *At Odds: Women and the Family in America from the Revolution to the Present* (New York, 1980), p. vii.

21. *Ibid.*, p. 472.

22. *Ibid.*, pp. 344, 345.

23. Lois W. Banner, *Women in Modern America: A Brief History* (New York, 1974), p. 2.

24. *Ibid.*, pp. 101–2.

25. *Ibid.*, p. 110.

26. As quoted in Banner, *Women in Modern America*, p. 114.

27. *Ibid.*, p. 115.

28. William L. O'Neill, *Everyone Was Brave: The Rise and Fall of Feminism in America* (Chicago, 1969).

29. As quoted in Degler, *At Odds*, p. 444.

30. *Cal. Fed. Savings and Loan Assn. v. Guerra*, 107 S.Ct.683 (1987).

31. Christine Curtis, "For Equality of the Sexes," *The California Lawyer*, June 1985, p. 16.

32. *Cal. Fed. Savings and Loan Assn. v. Guerra*.

33. Degler, *At Odds*, p. 466.

34. *Ibid.*, p. 360.

35. *Ibid.*, p. 461.

36. *New York Times*, Mar. 15, 1986, p. 3.

37. Ravi Batra, "Are the Rich Getting Richer?," *New York Times,* May 3, 1987.

2. NO-FAULT DIVORCE: THE EGALITARIAN TRIUMPH

1. U.S. Commission on Civil Rights Report, 1984, as quoted in *Newsweek,* July 15, 1985.
2. Not all single-parent homes are the casualty of divorce; many are the result of unwed mothers. The number of unwed mothers who apply for AFDC has increased rapidly also.
3. *Wall Street Journal,* Jan. 21, 1985, p. 12.
4. As of this writing South Dakota is still a holdout state.
5. Doris Jonas Freed and Henry H. Foster, "Family Law in the Fifty States: An Overview," *Family Law Quarterly* 17 (Winter 1984), pp. 373–75.
6. *Ibid.,* pp. 382–85.
7. California Civil Code, Sections 4000–5174.
8. Lenore J. Wietzman, *The Divorce Revolution* (New York, 1985), p. 225.
9. Freed and Foster, "Family Law in the Fifty States," pp. 383–88.
10. *New York Times,* Aug. 23, 1987.
11. California Civil Code, Section 4801(a).
12. *Wall Street Journal,* Jan. 21, 1985, p. 12.
13. "Pension Rights Division on Dissolution," 94ALR3d 176; Freed and Foster, "Family Law in the Fifty States."
14. Lenore J. Weitzman, "The Economics of Divorce: Social and Economic Consequences of Property, Alimony and Child Support Awards," *UCLA Law Review* 28 (1981), p. 1222.
15. Her real name and some of the facts have been altered at her request.
16. California Civil Code, Section 4800.3.
17. Weitzman, "The Economics of Divorce," p. 1266.
18. *Ibid.,* p. 1263.
19. California Civil Code, Section 4801(a)(5).
20. Public Hearings, "The Feminization of Poverty," California Assembly Art Agnos, California Assembly Human Services Committer, Apr. 8, 1983, pp. 158–59.
21. *New York Times,* Aug. 5, 1985, p. 1.
22. *Skinner v. Oklahoma,* 316 U.S. 533 (1942).
23. Carl Degler, *At Odds: Women and the Family in America*

from the Revolution to the Present (New York, 1980), pp. 5, 8.
24.   Freed and Foster, "Family Law in the Fifty States," p. 366.

3. SOLOMON'S SOLUTION: JOINT CUSTODY

1.   Doris Jonas Freed and Henry H. Foster, "Family Law in the Fifty States: An Overview," *Family Law Quarterly* 17 (Winter 1984), p. 369.
2.   As quoted in *Ms.*, Apr. 1983, p. 77.
3.   Lenore J. Weitzman, *The Marriage Contract* (New York, 1981), p. 145.
4.   California Civil Code, Sections 4600, 4600.5.
5.   *In re Marriage of Wood*, 141 Cal. App. 3d 671 (1982).
6.   *Dodd v. Dodd*, 403 N.Y.S. 2d 401, 93 Misc. 2d. 641 (1978).
7.   Currently there are a small handful of studies on the effects of voluntary joint custody on children. There are *no* studies of the effect of imposed rather than voluntary joint custody. The best study to date on voluntary joint custody is Steinman, "Joint Custody: What We Know, What We Have Yet to Learn, and the Judicial and Legislative Implications," 16 *UCD Law Review* 739 (1983).
8.   Judith S. Wallerstein and Joan Berlin Kelly, *Surviving the Breakup* (New York, 1980), p. 310.
9.   Dr. Judith Wallerstein, as quoted in *Ms.*, Apr. 1983, p. 77.
10.   *In Marriage of Burham*, 283 NW2d 269 (1979).
11.   Joseph Goldstein, Anna Freud, and Albert Solnit, *Beyond the Best Interests of the Child* (New York, 1973), p. 38.
12.   Weitzman, *The Marriage Contract*, p. 100.
13.   As quoted in *The Marriage Contract*, p. 101.
14.   See discussion in *The Marriage Contract*, p. 142.
15.   *Newsweek*, July 15, 1985.
16.   Lenore J. Weitzman, *The Divorce Revolution* (New York, 1985), p. 233.
17.   *Ibid.*, p. 244.
18.   David Chambers, "Re-thinking the Substantive Rules for Custody Disputes in Divorce," 83 *Mich. Law Review* 477 (1984).
19.   *Ibid.*, p. 544.
20.   *Ibid.*, p. 566.
21.   Shirley A. Settle and Carol Lowery, "Child Custody Decisions: Content Analysis of a Judicial Survey," *Journal of Divorce*, Vol. 6, No. 2 (Winter 1982), p. 137.

22. California Civil Code, Section 5180.
23. Interview with Dr. Judith Wallerstein.
24. *Ibid.*
25. *New York Times,* Oct. 22, 1986, p. 5.
26. *Ibid.*
27. Wallerstein and Kelly, *Surviving the Breakup,* pp. 43, 44.
28. As quoted in *Newsweek,* July 15, 1985.
29. Wallerstein and Kelly, *Surviving the Breakup,* p. 47.
30. *New York Times,* July 8, 1985.
31. Irvin Garfinkel and Elizabeth Lear, "A New Approach to Child Support," *Public Interest,* Spring 1984, p. 113.
32. Bureau of the Census, U.S. Department of Commerce, "Divorce, Child Custody, and Child Support," Census Population Reports, Series P.23, Nov. 1984.
33. Garfinkel and Lear, "A New Approach to Child Support," p. 114.
34. *Ibid.*
35. California Civil Code, Section 4701(a).
36. *New York Times,* Aug. 23, 1987.
37. Lenore J. Weitzman, "The Economics of Divorce: Social and Economic Consequences of Property, Alimony and Child Support Awards," *UCLA Law Review* 28 (1981), p. 1251.
38. Ruth Sidell, *Women and Children Last* (New York, 1986), p. 84.
39. *Ibid.,* p. 85.
40. Valerie Lezin, "Enforcing Child Support Orders," *California Lawyer* (Oct. 1986), p. 39.

4. WHY WOMEN WORK

1. Victor R. Fuchs, "Sex Differences in Economic Well-Being," *Science* 232 (Apr. 1986), p. 460; *Business Week,* Jan. 28, 1985, p. 81.
2. *Ibid., Business Week,* p. 80.
3. *Ms.,* July 1984, p. 60.
4. Ruth Sidell, *Women and Children Last* (New York, 1986), p. 61.
5. *Ibid.,* p. 66.
6. Maxine L. Margolis, *Mothers and Such* (Berkeley, 1984), p. 229.
7. Frank Levy, "Actually We Are All Getting Poorer," *New York Times,* May 3, 1987.

8. United States Department of Labor, "Perspectives on Working Women: A Datebook" (Washington, D.C., 1980), p. 4.

9. Maxine L. Margolis, *Mothers and Such* (Berkeley, 1984), p. 225.

10. *Ibid.*, p. 229.

11. *Ibid.*, p. 210.

12. *Ibid.*, p. 215.

13. Fuchs, "Sex Differences in Economic Well-Being," p. 461.

14. As quoted in Betty Friedan, *The Feminine Mystique* (New York, 1963), p. 17.

15. Jessie Bernard, *The Future of Marriage* (New York, 1972).

16. Joan Vanek, "Housewives as Workers," in *Women Working,* ed. Ann H. Stromberg and Shirley Harkess (Palo Alto, 1978), p. 404.

17. Keith Lane, "How Do You Put a Price Tag on a Housewife's Work?" *New York Times,* Jan. 13, 1976.

18. Ivan Illich, *Gender* (New York, 1982), p. 57.

5. WHY WOMEN EARN BOTTOM DOLLAR

1. There is continuing controversy about this figure. The Rand Study in 1985 reported that the gap was narrowing and women now earned 62 cents for every male dollar. In that same year the National Research Council, in "Women's Work, Men's Work: Sex Segregation on the Job," reported the figure as 59 cents to the dollar.

2. "Money, Income and Poverty Studies of Families in the U.S.," *Current Population Reports* (Washington, D.C.: Bureau of the Census, 1987) reported 70 cents for every male dollar. None of these studies, however, takes into consideration the huge numbers of women who work part time. This would lower the figure considerably.

3. Sylvia Hewlett, *A Lesser Life* (New York, 1985), p. 74.

4. *Ibid.*, p. 73.

5. Carl Degler, *At Odds* (New York, 1980), p. 426.

6. Mary Huff Stevenson, "Wage Differences between Men and Women: Economic Theories," in *Women Working,* ed. Ann H. Stromberg and Shirley Harkess (Palo Alto, 1978), p. 97.

7. Hewlett, *A Lesser Life*, p. 74.

8. *New York Times,* Mar. 15, 1986, p. 3.

9. Monica B. Morris, "Inequalities in the Labor Force," in *Women Working*, p. 168.

10. Ruth Sidell, *Women and Children Last* (New York, 1986), p. 197.

11. *Cal. Fed. Savings and Loan Assn. v. Guerra*, 107 S.Ct. 683 (1987).

12. *New York Times*, July 12, 1985, p. 2.

13. Gary Rosenberger, "Letting in Latchkey Children," *New York Times*, Aug. 11, 1985, "Education," p. 14.

14. Kenneth Keniston and the Carnegie Council for Children, *All My Children: The American Family Under Pressure* (New York, 1977), p. 9.

15. As quoted in Betty Friedan, *The Second Stage* (New York, 1981), p. 120.

16. Carolyn Teich Adams and Kathryn Winston, *Mothers at Work* (New York, 1980), p. 64.

17. *Ibid.*

18. *Ibid.*, p. 67.

19. *Ibid.*, p. 66.

20. *Ibid.*

21. As quoted in Maxine Margolis, *Mothers and Such* (Berkeley, 1984), p. 71.

22. *Ibid.*, p. 87.

23. *Ibid.*, p. 90.

24. *New York Times*, July 12, 1985, p. 22.

25. *Ibid.*, June 21, 1985, p. 25.

26. Adams and Winston, *Mothers at Work*, p. 28.

27. Sidell, *Women and Children Last*, p. 181.

28. Hewlett, *A Lesser Life*, p. 125.

29. Sidell, *Women and Children Last*, p. 131.

30. Hewlett, *A Lesser Life*, p. 130.

31. *San Francisco Chronicle*, June 20, 1986.

32. Sidell, *Women and Children Last*, p. 131.

33. Hewlett, *A Lesser Life*, p. 128.

6. WOMEN WHO LIVE TO WORK

1. Jane Gross, "Against the Odds: A Woman's Ascent on Wall Street," *New York Times Magazine*, Jan. 6, 1986, p. 19.

2. *Ibid.*

3. *Ibid.*, p. 22.

4. Geraldine Ferraro, *My Story* (New York, 1985), p. 54.

5. BBC interview with Margaret Thatcher, Nov. 24, 1985.

6. *San Francisco Examiner*, Jan. 27, 1985, p. 1.

7. *Ibid.*, p. A18.
8. Gross, "Against the Odds"; and *New York Times*, Nov. 25, 1984, p. 18.
9. Kati Morton in *New York Times*, June 12, 1985.
10. Cynthia Fuchs Epstein, *Women in Law* (New York, 1983), p. 16.
11. *Ibid.*, p. 366.
12. As quoted by Sandra Day O'Connor in *New York State Bar Journal* 6 (Oct. 1985), p. 9.
13. As quoted in Patricia Gerald Bourne and Norma Juliet Wikler, "Women in the Occupational World: Social Disruption and Conflict," in Rachel Kohn-Hut, Arlene Kaplon Daniels and Richard Calvard, eds., *Women and Work* (New York, 1982), p. 118.
14. Association of American Medical Colleges, *Medical School Requirements* (Washington, D.C., 1986).
15. Interview with Dr. Judith Kelleman, Berkeley, Calif., Jan. 1986.
16. As quoted in Kohn-Hut, Daniels and Calvard, *Women and Work*, p. 117.
17. Michelle Patterson and Laurie Engelberg, "Women in Male-Dominated Professions," in Ann Stromberg and Shirley Harkess, eds., *Women Working* (Palo Alto, 1978), p. 270.
18. Lois Banner, *Women in Modern America: A Brief History* (New York, 1974), p. 48.
19. Carl Degler, *At Odds* (New York, 1980), pp. 384–85.
20. Banner, *Women in Modern America*, p. 48.
21. *Ibid.*, pp. 103–4.
22. *The Recorder*, Apr. 25, 1986.
23. *Bakke v. Bd. of Regents* (1978), 438 U.S. 193.
24. Eva Jefferson Patterson, "The Future of Affirmative Action," *California Lawyer*, Vol. 6, No. 2, Feb. 1986.
25. As quoted in the *San Francisco Chronicle*, Mar. 26, 1987, p. 1.
26. As quoted in the *New York Times*, Mar. 29, 1987.

7. WOMEN WHO WORK TO LIVE

1. Frank Levy, "Actually We Are All Getting Poorer," *New York Times*, Mar. 3, 1987.
2. Studs Terkel, *Working* (New York, 1972), p. 59.
3. *Ibid.*, p. 5.

4. Shirley Hellsman Baker, "Women in Blue Collar and Service Occupations," in Ann Stromberg and Shirley Harkess, eds., *Women Working*, (Palo Alto, 1978), p. 346.

5. *Ibid.*, p. 350.

6. *Ibid.*, p. 351.

7. Carl Degler, *At Odds* (New York, 1980), p. 399.

8. Lois Banner, *Women in Modern America* (New York, 1974), p. 69.

9. Degler, *At Odds*, p. 401.

10. *Ibid.*

11. Baker, "Women Blue Collar and Service Occupations," p. 358.

12. James J. Kenneally, *Women and American Trade Unions* (Montreal, 1981), p. 198.

13. *Ibid.*, p. 201.

14. Larry S. Adams, "Changing Employment Patterns of Organized Workers," *Monthly Labor Review* (Feb. 1985), p. 25.

15. As quoted in Pamela Roby, "The Conditions of Women in Blue Collar, Industrial and Service Jobs: A Review of Research and Proposals for Action and Policy" (New York, Russell Sage Foundation), p. 64.

16. Kenneally, *Women and American Trade Unions*, p. 192.

17. Terkel, *Working*, p. 91.

18. Roberta Goldberg, *Organizing Women Office Workers* (New York, 1983), p. 33.

19. *Ibid.*, p. 25.

20. Ronnie Steinberg and Lars Hargnere, "Separate but Equivalent Equal Pay for Work of Comparable Worth," in *Gender at Work*, publication of the Women's Research and Education Institute of the Congressional Caucus for Women's Issues (Washington, D.C., 1984), p. 25.

21. *AFSCME v. State of Washington*, 578 F. Supp 846 (WD Washington, 1983).

22. *AFSCME v. State of Washington*, 770 F.2d. 140 (1985).

23. *New York Times*, January 27, 1986.

24. California Government Code, Section 1982.2.

25. Fred E. Katz, "Nurses," in *The Semi-Professions and Their Organization*, ed. Amitai Etzioni (New York, 1972), p. 61.

8. THE INVISIBLE MAJORITY:
REENTRY AND PART-TIME WORKERS

1. U.S. Bureau of Labor Statistics Employment and Earnings Monthly, Mar. 1984. This figure, based on the 1975 census, counts as full-time workers women who work 35 hours or more each week the year round.
2. Alice M. Yohalem, *Women Returning to Work* (New Jersey, 1980), pp. 243, 244.
3. *Ibid.*, p. 263.
4. As quoted in *Women Returning to Work*, p. 258.
5. Yohalem, *Women Returning to Work*, p. 257.
6. Lillian Rubin, *Women of a Certain Age* (New York, 1979), p. 180.
7. *Ibid.*, p. 181.
8. Displaced Homemakers' Center, 1515 Webster Street, Room 431, Oakland, Calif.
9. Ruth Sidell, *Women and Children Last* (New York, 1986), p. 161.
10. Aileen Applebaum, *Back to Work* (Boston, 1981), p. 103.
11. *Ibid.*, p. 102.
12. *Ibid.*

9. WOMEN'S RIGHTS AND WOMEN'S VISIONS

1. "Households, Families, Marital Status and Living Arrangements" (March 1987 Advance Report), as reported in the *San Francisco Chronicle*, Sept. 10, 1987.
2. Geraldine Ferraro, *Ferraro: My Story* (New York, 1985), p. 136.

INDEX

CALIFORNIA COLLEGE OF ARTS & CRAFTS

I CAC 00 0060745 V

RESERVE

Fall '97

BRODART, INC.   Cat. No. 23 233   Printed in U.S.A.